THE LAWS OF COMMUNICATION
[FOR PREACHING]

The Laws of Communication (for Preaching)

Unless otherwise noted, all Scripture quotations are taken from the HCSB®, Copyright © 1999, 2000, 2002, 2003, 2009 by Holman Bible Publishers. Used by permission. HCSB® is a federally registered trademark of Holman Bible Publishers.

Scriptures marked KJV are taken from the KING JAMES VERSION (KJV): KING JAMES VERSION, public domain.

Scripture quotations marked TPT are from The Passion Translation®. Copyright © 2017 by BroadStreet Publishing® Group, LLC. Used by permission. All rights reserved. ThePassionTranslation.com.

Scripture quotations taken from the Amplified® Bible (AMP), Copyright © 2015 by The Lockman Foundation. Used by permission. www.Lockman.org

ISBN: 9781980939412

Copyright © 2018 by David Snyder

All rights reserved. No part of this book may be reproduced or transmitted in any form or by any means, electronic or mechanical, including photocopying and recording, or by any informational storage and retrieval system, without permission in writing from the publisher.

BubbaBooks Publishing

CONTENTS

Introduction 9

Chapter 1: The Law of the Boiler 14
Our outward lives are a reflection of our time in the presence of God

Chapter 2: The Law of Direction 24
You can't lead where you haven't been

Chapter 3: The Law of John Wayne 33
Fear must be faced head on

Chapter 4: The Law of the Bridge 41
Communication is earned through bridge building

Chapter 5: The Law of Engagement 49
Effective communication demands that an audience be fully engaged

Chapter 6: The Law of the Dreamer 59
Imagine what your message could look like

Chapter 7: The Law of the Listener 68

You will become like what you consistently listen to

Chapter 8: The Law of the Spear 77

Every good sermon must have a point, if not it will be dull and useless

Chapter 9: The Law of Chewing the Cud ... 86

Find your message early and chew on it

Chapter 10: The Law of the Tee Off 96

If you want people to listen you must start well

Chapter 11: The Law of The Big Picture 105

Good communicators don't just speak, they paint a picture

Chapter 12: The Law of the Mirror 113

Hold up a mirror for people to see that the message is for them

Chapter 13: The Law of the Catalyst 121

Preaching should lead people to change

Chapter 14: The Law of Hope 130
Don't forget the good in the good news

Chapter 15: The Law of the Drill 137
Communication takes practice

Chapter 16: The Law of Delivery 146
Good communication comes through good delivery

Chapter 17: The Law of Review 154
Communication improves with regular review

Chapter 18: The Law of Growth 164
Don't just survive, learn to thrive

Chapter 19: The Law of the Bell 173
Good communicators become great with time, never give up

Thank You 183
Appendix 185
Notes 188

INTRODUCTION

The noise of the train rumbled in the man's ears, lulling him to sleep. It was after midnight and he was tired and bored. His job was to wait for the train and warn traffic to avoid any accidents. The problem was there was never any traffic in the small town in the middle of the night.

The man sat at his post fighting sleep while the train passed until he saw something approaching. He rubbed his eyes; he wasn't dreaming, a car was approaching. Without a second thought he grabbed his lantern and waved it to warn the driver. But the car kept coming.

He shouted now and waved the lantern even faster. The driver kept speeding toward the train. A moment later it was over. The driver and everyone in the car with him were dead. They didn't notice the man with the lantern.

The police came to investigate.

"Were you in your booth watching for traffic before the vehicle arrived?" the detective asked.

"Did you see the vehicle approaching?"

"Yes."

"Did you wave your lantern to warn the driver?"

"Yes."

"Well, it appears you did everything right. You were not at fault. The driver just didn't slow down."

"No," the man replied. "You're just not asking the right questions. I waved my lantern the way I should have. But I hadn't even noticed my light had gone out."

The lantern man had one job. He needed to communicate with drivers. He thought he was doing everything right, but the driver didn't get the message. There was a breakdown in the communication.

"COMMUNICATION WORKS FOR THOSE WHO WORK AT IT."

-John Powell

Let's be honest, communication is tough. It takes a lot of work to communicate ideas and thoughts in a way that people will understand and relate to. But sometimes our messages seem to fall on deaf ears. We wonder, why don't they listen? Maybe they are not the problem. Could it be there is a failure to communicate? Somewhere down the line the message is getting lost. We need to figure out where the problem is and deal with it.

We communicate every day but why is it some people seem to be better at it than others. Those who have learned, by hard work and practice, to become better communicators reap the reward. For those who communicate well in a marriage relationship, the reward is a healthy marriage. Those who communicate well in their jobs often see the reward of promotion and/or increased sales. For those of us who preach the Gospel few things are more important than good communication. The reward is obvious, people will come to know Jesus and have an opportunity for a deep relationship with Him.

Communication is the goal of preaching. We are not speaking to the air. We are speaking to be heard. Becoming a great communicator isn't just for a chosen few. I believe everyone has potential to become a world-class communicator and preacher. My prayer is that this book will give you the tools you need to communicate the Gospel well.

Let me make a disclaimer, I am not trying to bill myself as a communication or preaching guru. I do my best and God is faithful. Honestly, some of my messages are better than others but I am always trying to improve. I want to continue growing and the Lord knows I have room for improvement, but I have also learned a few things over two decades of preaching.

In the pages that follow you will encounter the Laws of Communication. Laws must be obeyed. There are laws that govern every area of our lives, like driving a car or building a house. Just like breaking the law when driving can lead to an accident, and breaking a law while building a house can cause problems down the road, breaking a law of communication will lead to a failure in the message.

Some will want to argue these laws. They might say, "Preaching is an art. There are no laws in art. Preach however you want."

My goal is not to squash creativity. These laws allow for freedom to preach creatively. In fact I would say they encourage it. But they have to do with how we communicate. Preaching is communicating and we have an obligation to communicate effectively.

Some might argue, "I don't need to follow any laws. I just let the Holy Spirit lead me."

"IF YOU JUST COMMUNICATE YOU CAN GET BY. BUT IF YOU COMMUNICATE SKILLFULLY YOU CAN WORK MIRACLES."

-Jim Rohn

Just like creativity, I am 100% for letting the Holy Spirit lead us. The Holy Spirit can lead us as we prepare to preach as well as He can while we preach. We should never use the Holy Spirit as an excuse to be unprepared.

I don't want to suggest that this is all about us and ignore the work of the Holy Spirit. But we are entrusted with the most important message on this planet. In fact we have the most important job on the planet. We have a responsibility to communicate this message clearly and let the Holy Spirit do his work.

Preaching is communicating Jesus to the world. If you follow these laws, it will help you to be prepared, communicate clearly and capture the attention of those you are ministering to. The rest is up to Him.

No matter where you are on your journey, whether you are just starting out or if you have been preaching for many years, I hope you find encouragement and practical help to become all that God has called you to be.

Some laws deal with you as a person and developing the right heart and attitude before you step in the pulpit. Other laws deal with putting your sermon together and are designed to help you as you prepare your message. And others are about helping you connect with your audience and deliver the message the best way possible.

At the end of each chapter you'll find suggestions to help you put the law into practice. I would suggest you make notes as you read and try to incorporate a few ideas each time you write and deliver a sermon. So let's get right into it.

When you finish reading this if you find you need more specific help or have questions please feel free to contact me. Also I've put together a video series based on this book. You can watch the videos or reach me through my website at: **lawsofcommunication.weebly.com**

THE LAW OF THE BOILER

Our outward lives and ministry are a reflection of our time in the presence of God

I heard a story of a town that had been dry for years until a man came and opened a bar. A group of concerned Christians got together to pray against the bar, asking God to intervene. Not long after the prayer meeting lightning hit the bar and it burnt to the ground. The bar owner took the group of Christians to court and sued them for destroying his business. The Christians hired a lawyer and argued in court that there was no way they could be held responsible. They claimed they had nothing to do with lightning striking his building.

After the judge heard the opening arguments, he sat back and made this observation, "No matter how this case comes out, one thing is clear. The bar owner believes in prayer and the Christians do not."[1]

Now that may not be a true story but the fact

remains, many Christians simply do not believe in prayer. I don't mean they don't believe in praying but they don't believe their prayers do anything. That may sound judgmental and I'm not trying to be. But I wonder, if we believed in prayer like we said we did, wouldn't we pray more? If we really believed in prayer wouldn't we pray differently?

What's the point? I'm talking about your prayer life. I know, you've heard it before. It might be tempting to skip this chapter but don't do it! This one law is the hinge on which swings every aspect of your life and ministry. I can't oversell it. If we don't have this one law at work in our lives, we might as well quit.

"A PREPARED MESSENGER IS MORE IMPORTANT THAN A PREPARED MESSAGE."
-Robert Munger

So what is it? The Law of the Boiler states that our outward lives and ministry will be a reflection of our time spent in the presence of God. It is in His presence where the fire of Holy Spirit is stirred.

There is a story about some young college students who came to visit the church where Charles Spurgeon was pastoring. These students came early and waited outside for the service to begin. After a while a man noticed them standing around.

"Gentlemen, let me show you around," the man offered.

The boys followed the big man. They wondered if he was the janitor. The man began his tour by taking them down into the basement of the church.

"Would you like to see the heating plant of this church?" the man asked.

The boys weren't interested, not to mention it was the middle of the summer, but they didn't want to be rude so they nodded.

They walked to the end of the hall. The boys could hear a sound coming from behind a door. Was the boiler running in the middle of the summer?

The man pushed the door open. The boys leaned inside and saw about seven hundred people gathered praying.

"This is our heating plant," the man whispered as he closed the door.

The man was Charles Spurgeon. He knew the power of prayer.

We'd all agree prayer is important. It's vital. It's foundational to what we believe. We agree that it is the cornerstone to our relationship with God. Most of us would probably acknowledge that we should pray more.

The question is why don't we?

This world is desperate for a genuine encounter with God. We need to be so filled with Him that He spills out of us, not only when we preach but also when we are outside our churches. We owe this world an encounter with God.

FROM GLORY TO GLORY

Prayer is the key that opens the door for everything you need in your life and ministry. Without a prayer life we're just teaching an empty religion. Your prayer life is the connection to the heart of God. The time you spend in prayer is developing your personal, intimate relationship with the Father. If we are lacking this area, our preaching will lack the passion that comes from intimacy. It's like switching on the thermostat but not getting any heat. You've got to have the pilot light on. If there is no fire, there is no heat.

Someone once said, "Get on fire for God and people will come to watch you burn." Our hearts need to be set ablaze with a love for God that overflows from our time with Him. The people who come to your church need to experience a real encounter with God. This generation is hungry for something genuine. They don't want to hear an empty, powerless message. Instead they long for someone to show them a passionate, powerful relationship with God is possible.

I'm not suggesting you should get worked up into some kind of emotionalism when you preach. Again if it's fake, no one is interested. What I am getting at is that your intimacy with the Father will spill out of you when you preach. You won't be able to help it. The time spent with Him in private will spill out of you in public.

When Moses came down off the mountain, his face was glowing. Imagine what that must have been like to see Moses glowing. He must have been brighter than those glow in the dark things kids stick on their ceilings because they could see him in the daytime too. People saw him and it scared them to death. They made him wear a veil on his face because they were so freaked out about it.[2]

Paul contrasts the experience Moses had to our lives in Christ. He says Moses' glory was fading but we are going from glory to glory.[3] We have an even greater glory than Moses did because we have greater access to the Father through the blood of Jesus. Think about that. The intimate relationship Moses had is nothing compared to what you and I have. Moses couldn't look at God's face. He could get close to God but not too close. But we have the very Spirit of God living on the inside of us. Moses had to climb a mountain to be near God but God lives in us.

As we spend time with Him, we will not be able to help reflect His glory. As we preach people will see that in our lives. They will hear it in our words. We talk sometimes about the anointing. People pray for an anointing to preach or do a certain thing. I believe in the anointing but I wonder if we have a bad understanding of it.

In the Old Testament people had the anointing come on them at different times for certain tasks. The Holy Spirit would come on them for a time and then He would leave. We don't have that kind of anointing. Because of what Jesus has done for us we don't need to strive to get an anointing to preach a message and then work to get more anointing for the next one. We already have His anointing. We can walk in that anointing. The Holy Spirit lives in us. Notice what it says in Romans 8:11,

> *And if the Spirit of Him who raised Jesus from the dead lives in you, then He who raised Christ from the dead will also bring*

your mortal bodies to life through His Spirit who lives in you.

It's the same Spirit. His Holy Spirit is living in you. The same Spirit that made Christ to triumph over death, hell and the grave is inside you. You have the same Spirit. He is the third person of the trinity and He has taken up residence in you and He will give life to your body. He will make your body come alive with His life. You don't have to ask for an anointing, you already have it! All you need is walk in the anointing you have. That only comes through being with Him.

"PRAYER WILL SINGULARLY ASSIST YOU IN THE DELIVERY OF YOUR SERMON; IN FACT, NOTHING CAN SO GLORIOUSLY FIT YOU TO PREACH AS DESCENDING FRESH FROM THE MOUNT OF COMMUNION WITH GOD TO SPEAK WITH MEN."
-Charles Spurgeon

ALL TRUTH

In case that wasn't enough, it is but let's go with it for a minute, there's another reason to develop your prayer life. As you pray the Holy Spirit will lead you and guide you into ALL TRUTH. See sometimes we think we know the right thing, we think we know what's good for us, but just because it seems good doesn't mean it's God. It might look good and smell good but it could be the wrong thing. In John 16:13, Jesus says,

> *Yet when the Spirit of Truth comes, he'll guide you into all truth. He won't speak on his own accord, but he'll speak whatever he hears and will declare to you the things that are to come.*

How can we possibly know what to do? The Holy Spirit always knows the answer. He is your cheat sheet. All we have to do is ask Him. If we ask, He will guide us into all truth. You can know what to do with every decision that comes your way. The Holy Spirit will guide you into ALL truth. Every financial decision, every opportunity, everything, He will guide you. It says in Proverbs 3:5 that if we "acknowledge Him in all our ways He will direct our paths." The key to being led in all truth is acknowledging Him. He can't guide us if we don't ask. But as we develop our prayer time we learn to ask and listen.

As you pray, He will prompt you about things that are coming. Notice that verse again in John 16. It says, "He will declare to you the things that are to come." What are things to come? That's anything coming up in your life you need to know about, anything you need to be prepared for. But again, it comes through intimacy, taking time to listen to His voice.

"GOD SPEAKS IN THE SILENCE OF THE HEART. LISTENING IS THE BEGINNING OF PRAYER."
                                              -Mother Teresa

I spoke to a Pastor from Haiti several years ago. It was a couple of years after the terrible earthquake that devastated the country. He told me about what happened to his son during the earthquake. His son was sitting in school minding his own business when suddenly there was a voice behind him that shouted, "Get out!"

He just about jumped out of his seat. When he looked behind him there was no one there. Then he heard the voice a second time even louder, "GET OUT NOW!" He stood up in the middle of class and grabbed his bag. His friend asked him what he was doing. He said, "I'm getting out of here." His friend probably thought he was ditching school, so he said, "I'm going too." Together they ran out of the school. Several minutes later the earthquake hit and the school collapsed. The Holy Spirit told him things that were to come.

As you walk out the Law of the Boiler, God will move in new and powerful ways in your life and ministry. Hebrews 11:6 says,

> *Now without faith it is impossible to please God, for the one who draws near to Him must believe that He exists and rewards those who seek Him.*

The two key elements of faith. 1. You must believe that God exists. 2. You must believe that He is a rewarder of those who seek Him. In the King James it says, "diligently seek." There are those who seek God and then there are those who seek Him diligently. Let's be the kind of people who seek Him diligently. We can't preach someone we don't know.

He will bless your life and ministry as you apply the Law of the Boiler and seek Him.

NUTS & BOLTS

- *Block out a prayer time in your schedule (if you don't already have one).*

  This is a time that will not be interrupted by anything other than an emergency. This is solely time for you and your relationship with God. Yes we are to pray without ceasing. Prayer can and should happen all the time. But this is a time dedicated to seeking God.

- *Start a prayer journal*

  This is going to help you zero in on what you are praying about and help you keep a record of your thoughts of what God is speaking to you for your life and ministry.

  Write something in the journal every day. Record things like: what you are praying for, what you feel God is speaking to you, verses that stand out as you do your Bible reading, etc.

- *Build a worship routine*

  Make worship part of your prayer routine. Spend time in praise and thanksgiving. Not only is it pleasing to God but also it is where victories happen in your life.

THE LAW OF DIRECTION
You can't lead where you haven't been

"Follow me. I know the way."

- Marcus Brody

    One of my favorite movies of all time is Indiana Jones and the Last Crusade. What kid in the 80's didn't wish they had a Fedora and bullwhip? At least I know this kid did. Indiana Jones was an icon for adventure. Nothing says you've got it together like wearing a heavy leather jacket while digging for artifacts in the Middle East. If anyone knew where he was going it was Indiana Jones.

    There's a character in the movie named, Marcus Brody. He is in charge of the museum that funds Indiana Jones' adventures. He's also a goofy guy. At one point Indiana tells his father that Marcus once got lost in his own museum. At the end of the movie as Indiana, his father and Marcus are about to ride off into the sunset, Marcus yells, "Indy, Henry, follow me. I know the way." He nearly falls off his horse as he rides off.

In life and in ministry there are people like Indiana and people like Marcus. Some have clear direction, others think they do. We might think we know the way or think we know what to do but there is a difference between doing what seems right and doing what God is calling us to. It's like a man with a broken compass walking in circles and thinking he's making progress.

The Law of Direction is about helping you to understand where you are going in life and ministry. Without direction from the Lord you're just wandering through life. The Law of Direction can be summed up with this, "Seek the Lord for direction in your life and you'll avoid getting lost."

I can guess what you're thinking. "Great advice. But what does this have to do with preaching?"

I'm glad you asked. When we have a clear direction for our lives and ministries our preaching should help to drive the vision home. But you must first start with a vision to know where God wants to take the people. Your sermon is an avenue to help people get to their destination. Without direction people will feel lost. That doesn't mean all of your sermons have to be about one central theme. But it means in many of your sermons that theme will pop up.

START WITH YOU

Let me ask you this question: Where are you going? Do you have a clear direction for your own life? As a preacher there is a responsibility to lead people, it's in the job description. You could become the greatest speaker in the world but if you don't learn how to live what you're preaching it's all been for nothing. If you look and sound like you have it all together but you're just stumbling through life like Marcus Brody, no one will care what you have to say.

"IT IS NO USE WALKING ANYWHERE TO PREACH UNLESS OUR WALKING IS OUR PREACHING."
-St. Francis of Assisi

No please don't misunderstand me. I'm not saying you need to be perfect to preach. We are all a work in progress. But if your life is not in order, you need to work on you before you step up to the pulpit. You should be able to say, like the Apostle Paul did, "Imitate me, as I also imitate Christ."[4]

Your life should have a clear direction. Before you can preach a vision for someone else, you need a vision for you. Many preachers seem willing to lay things on the altar of ministry that God never asked them to. In fact some might use the idea of sacrifice as an excuse for not working on some area they should be. For example, "God has called me to do ministry, so I don't have time to exercise." You need exercise. God wants you to exercise. Make time for it.

Some have done similar things with their marriages, their children, their finances, you name it. Their lives are not in order. We need to be people with a vision for our own lives. We need to see that God wants to work in every area of our lives, not just our preaching. If you burn out today you aren't any good tomorrow. We get into this more in a later chapter.

THE GAME CHANGER

Let's take this to a spiritual dimension. In the same way you need to have direction for your physical life, you also need direction in your spiritual life. This is a foundational law. Without this law in place and functioning in your life any preaching you do will be shallow. I can't oversell this. It's impossible to lead people where you haven't been. To communicate the Gospel, we must have more than just a working knowledge of God. We must have an intimate knowledge of Him.

Intimacy with God is the game changer. Imagine a man who lives deep in Amazon with a tribe, isolated from the outside world. One day a visitor comes and gives the man a magazine about cars. The man is thrilled. He reads every page and studies ever picture closely. The rest of the tribe learns of the man's enthusiasm and they want to hear more about it. The man holds a lecture to teach all about cars. He tells them about the new Camaro. He rattles off numbers he has memorized about the size of the engine and the miles per hour. But no one including him knows what any of that means. They have never heard of miles per hour and they don't know what an engine is.

Now imagine the difference if one day the man travels to a city and rides in a car. He hitches a ride in a convertible and can feel the wind in his hair. They show him how the car accelerates and point out the speedometer with the miles per hour. Suddenly he understands things he had been talking about. It's a game changer! Nothing he had said was wrong before. But to have a working knowledge of the car will help him be able to communicate so others will understand.

"I DON'T PRACTICE WHAT I PREACH, I PREACH WHAT I PRACTICE."

-Charles Capps

Look at what it says in 2 Peter 1:2-3

> *May grace and peace be multiplied to you through the knowledge of God and of Jesus our Lord. His divine power has given us everything required for life and godliness through the knowledge of Him who called us by His own glory and goodness.*

Notice the word knowledge pops up there twice. How does he say grace and peace are multiplied? It's through the knowledge of God. That's powerful stuff right there. Grace and peace. Grace is often a misunderstood word. So many people view that as just a covering for sin. The grace of God might do that but it's so much more. In some places it's translated as favor. God wants to show his favor to you. I heard someone give this definition of grace,

"God wants to treat you like sin never happened." So it's not just a covering, but it has to do with the way God views and treats us. And the word peace has to do with every area of our lives. It's not just an emotion, it's well being in every situation.

How does all that come? He says it comes through the knowledge of God.

But he goes on to say God's divine power has given us everything we need for life and for godliness. What do you need in life? It's taken care of. It's not just in the spiritual realm, that's there too. But it says life and godliness. What do you need in your ministry? You have it. What do you need to live a life that pleases God? Nothing. You already have it. His power that's at work in you by the Holy Spirit is giving you everything you need. Again, it comes through the knowledge of Him.

The word knowledge in this verse has nothing to do with book smarts. This isn't a word for going to college and cramming for a test so you know the answers. It's about intimate, first hand knowledge. It's the difference between reading about a car and driving in one.

If we are going to communicate the Gospel in a way that will draw people to have an intimate relationship with God, we must first have that intimacy ourselves. Again, you can't lead people where you haven't been. It's one thing to preach about it. But it's another to experience and then preach about it.

The man with experience will always trump the man with head knowledge.

LIVE BETTER THAN YOU PREACH

There was a bishop who lived in the last part of the 1800's and the early 1900's. In his time there were many people questioning if man could ever fly. Could someone build an airplane. Many were trying but all were failing. This preacher proclaimed from his pulpit it was impossible to construct a "heavier-than-air flight." Not only was it impossible, but he took it one step further and announced it was contrary to the will of God. This preacher also published a newsletter and repeated his claims.

It's ironic that the preacher had two sons who didn't listen to him. The man's name was Milton Wright and his two sons Orville and Wilbur went on to build the first airplane. Their father had no vision but his son's did. They could see farther down the road.[5]

Proverbs 29:18 gets quoted often but for good reason. It says, "Where there is no vision, the people perish." (KJV)

It's true. Without a vision you won't make it. In the book, *Alice in Wonderland*, there's a moment where Alice is lost and she meets the Cheshire Cat. She stops and asks the cat, "Would you tell me, please, which way I ought to go from here?"

The cat replies, "That depends a good deal on where you want to get to."

"I don't much care where."

"Then it doesn't much matter which way you go."[6]

We need to know where we are going. If you ask, Holy Spirit will lead you and guide you in all truth. It all comes back to that intimate knowledge. As you know Him he will lead you in the way you should go. What should I be doing in my ministry? He will lead you. What should I be preaching about? He will guide you.

Your preaching will flow out of an intimate knowledge of Him.

I work with college-age students in our ministry. Part of what we do is train them to preach. Occasionally one of them will call and ask for prayer because they are going to preach somewhere. I have started praying this prayer when they ask,

"Lord, let them live better than they preach."

It might irritate some of them. They might want me to pray for them to do a great job. I want them to succeed. But my definition of success goes beyond the border of the pulpit and extends out into their entire lives. My desire for them and my desire for myself is that I would live even better than I preach. That doesn't mean I don't want to do my best. I believe preaching is important, (I wrote a whole book about it!) But I want to live better.

It's nice to hear you did a good job preaching. We all like to hear encouraging words, it's better than being told you did lousy. But the greatest compliment any of us could ever receive is to hear that we live better than we preach. You might become one of the greatest speakers on this planet, may you live even better.

NUTS & BOLTS

- *Seek the Lord for direction in your life and ministry*

    Without a sense of direction people just float through life. Maybe you had direction at one time but now you feel like you're floating. Ask for fresh vision and direction. Where does the Lord want to take you personally in this next season of your life? Pray the same for your ministry.

- *Journal your direction*

    Write it down. The vision is just a good idea until you record it. Use your prayer journal or another journal and write down as much as you can about the direction you feel the Lord is taking you in. Review it and alter it as needed.

- *Share the vision*

    Now that you have direction for your life and for the ministry you are connected with, develop a list of sermon ideas connected with the vision. As you share and preach the vision people will come along with you to help make it happen.

THE LAW OF JOHN WAYNE
Fear must be faced head on

What do you do if one of the most powerful leaders in the world has sent assassins to kill you? Change your name? Run and hide? Beg for your life? Not if you're John Wayne. If you're John Wayne, you face it head on.

It might sound like something out of a movie but this happened to John Wayne. It was the height of the cold war and no one was as outspoken against the evils of communism as Wayne. He was just as outspoken against Joseph Stalin, the leader of the U.S.S.R. When Stalin heard about this outspoken actor who personified the American way of life, he decided to have him killed. He sent KGB agents with the sole purpose of taking out John Wayne.

John Wayne was not his real name by the way. It was a stage name. Everyone who knew him called him Duke. But Duke was not his real name. He had a dog named Duke. His real name was Marion Morrison. He hated his name. He got picked on as a kid because of his name and he grew up resenting it. When some firemen who knew him started calling his dog little Duke and called him big Duke, the name stuck. But the name John Wayne represented the characters he played. John Wayne was a tough-as-nails cowboy who never backed down from a fight. He was brave, courageous, and daring. Everything a young boy named Marion, and a man named Duke wanted to be.

> "COURAGE IS BEING SCARED TO DEATH BUT SADDLING UP ANYWAY."
>
> -John Wayne

When the FBI wanted to put John Wayne in protective custody he refused. Instead he enlisted his own spies, a group of Hollywood stuntmen, to infiltrate the communist groups around the city. They captured the hitmen with the help of the FBI. More assassins would come. John Wayne would survive attacks by KGB agents and a sniper sent by Mao, the communist leader of China. But he refused to back down. He never let fear control him. He was the brave cowboy in the end.[i]

For most people the controlling factor in their life is fear. Fear seems to make the world go round. Fear makes headlines every morning on the news cycle because fear keeps people tuned in.

I heard an ad for the local news once that ran

something like this, "Why the color yellow might be killing you… story at 11."

What?

Turns out there might be poison in the dye they use for yellow. Put down that highlighter.

Fear motivates people. Some people take a job they know they will hate out of fear.

"I'd like to do something else… but I'm afraid it might not work out."

Fear makes us do things we don't really want to do.

"I don't want to go to that party… but I'm afraid they'll think I don't like them."

It's the same with preaching. So many are terrified of preaching, or any kind of public speaking that they avoid it like the plague. Now if you're reading this and you've been preaching for a while this is something you've learned to overcome. But if you're starting out, maybe this has been a struggle you've had to face. You want to be in ministry, but you don't want to preach. You feel God has called you to preach but the idea scares you to death. Perhaps you have a few sermons under your belt and instead of growing confident you are more terrified. The thought of getting up to speak keeps you up at night.

The good news is, you are not alone.

I remember my first sermon. I was a wreck. My knees were shaking the whole time. I wish I could say the fear magically went away after that first time. It didn't. Around that same time I met a guy in Bible college who told me he wanted to be a pastor. Someone asked him about preaching and he said he didn't want to preach. He didn't like standing in front of people it scared him to death. I could relate to that. Preaching can be scary.

This is where the Law of John Wayne comes in. When that fear rises in you and wants to control you, the only thing you can do is get all John Wayne on that thing. If fear says to sit down and keep quiet, you just mosey on up and preach the Word. Fear might tell you, you can't. You stand up and say "I can do all things through Christ who gives me strength."

Even John Wayne wasn't really John Wayne. But it represented who he wanted to be. Who do you want to be? Don't get me wrong. I don't mean to imply that John Wayne was a godly person we should act like. He wasn't. But when a fear filled situation arose in his life, he faced it like the cowboy he played in the movies. He became John Wayne.

"SINCE IT IS SO LIKELY THAT CHILDREN WILL MEET CRUEL ENEMIES, LET THEM AT LEAST HAVE HEARD OF BRAVE KNIGHTS AND HEROIC COURAGE."

-C.S. Lewis

DON'T PLAY IT SAFE

Fear won't just go away. If you are struggling with fear in preaching or speaking the only thing you can do is face it head on. This goes for every area of our lives, not just preaching. Fear will control your life if you let it. The sad truth is many are not doing what they are called to do because fear is telling them to play it safe.

In Matthew 25, Jesus tells the parable of the talents. Remember the story? A man is going on a long trip, so he calls his servants and gives each of them some money. To one he gives five talents, another gets two and one gets one. There is some argument about how much money a talent was. Most scholars agree it was the largest value of money they had. Some have estimated the equivalent for a talent to be equal to 20 years wages. Today, with an average US salary, that would be about $1,000,000. No matter how you cut it that was a lot of money.

So the guy who had what we'll call five million, put his money to work. He was able to double it. The man with two million did the same thing and doubled his but the guy with one million dug a hole and buried his money.

When the master returned each one came and presented him with the fruit of their work. The first one said, "Master, here's your five million dollars back and look, I made five more."

The Master was pleased. "Well done, good and faithful servant." Then he makes a statement that should be the foundation for all of our lives. "You were faithful with small things, I will put you in charge of many things. Share in your Master's joy."

We all have to learn to be faithful with everything we are entrusted with. Sometimes we miss the small things because we are looking for big things. We need to do the small things well.

The second man comes, gives the master his two million dollars and the two extra he earned. The Master never criticizes him for not making as much as the first man. He never compares them. We would do that. "Why did that guy get five, and I only got two?" It's interesting, it says they were, "given according to their own abilities." That drives us crazy. Jealousy steps in all too easily. But let me stop preaching and get to the point.

The man with the one million dollars comes to the Master, look what he says, "Master, I know you are a difficult man..." (Not scoring any points here!) "So I was afraid and went off and hid your talent in the ground."

The parable of the talents ends badly for this guy. He winds up being tossed out into darkness where there is "weeping and gnashing of teeth." It would have been nice if the Master had come back and said, "There, there. You were scared weren't you. I know. Come here, it will be all right." But he calls him "worthless." Ouch.

What made him do it? Why didn't he use what he was entrusted with? FEAR. Fear controlled his life. Fear kept him from being productive. Fear kept him a prisoner. I can just imagine this guy digging the hole, looking around to be sure no one was watching. Then he probably set up camp over the money to guard it. I'm sure he took it seriously. He might have convinced himself he was doing a good job, not doing anything at all. He probably told himself this is what the Master would have wanted. Look the guy was only given one talent, and that was given according to his ability. Perhaps he looked at that and said, "I wasn't given what those other guys were. They have a much greater ability than me. If the Master really expected me to do something he would have given me more." And on it goes.

"THE FEAR OF DEATH FOLLOWS FROM THE FEAR OF LIFE. A MAN WHO LIVES FULLY IS PREPARED TO DIE AT ANY TIME."

-Mark Twain

We can fall into the same trap. "I'm not as talented a preacher as this other guy. That guy seems to have it all together. I just don't have that kind of ability." We always lose when we compare ourselves to others. You weren't called to be someone else. You were called to be you and to let Jesus shine through you. Don't let fear be a factor for you. (Yes that was a Fear Factor nod.)

Put the Law of John Wayne to work in your life and ministry. Whatever fear you might face whatever thing might stand in the way of you doing what God has called you to do, just cowboy up to that thing and face it head on.

NUTS & BOLTS

- *Evaluate: Fear Factor*

    Pray about your life and ministry. Has fear been a controlling factor in any part of it? Have you avoided preaching something because of what some people might think? Has fear kept you from chasing a dream? Determine to never let fear be factor in your life.

- *Plan*

    What would you do different this week (or month or year), if there was no fear of failure?

THE LAW OF THE BRIDGE
Communication is earned through bridge building

When I was in college a friend of mine was in charge of a ministry team that traveled to rodeos and held cowboy church. I wasn't interested and was already involved in several ministries so I didn't expect to join him on one of his trips. But one day his team was leaving, and I had a free weekend so I jumped in a car and we headed to Kansas City.

I had never been to a rodeo and no matter how hard I would have tried I could not have passed for a cowboy (I still can't). But the event and the culture impressed me. It was an exciting experience. Our team worked behind the scenes at the rodeo. At one point I met the Nitty Gritty Dirt Band, who I had never heard of but were apparently a big deal. On Sunday that weekend our main ministry took place. We were working with a rodeo chaplain who was in charge of the Cowboy Church.

What stands out in my memory the most was after the event. The chaplain came and spoke to our team; he scolded us for not looking like cowboys. Well, that was because we weren't. Most of the team looked like me: no boots, no cowboy hat and a small belt buckle.. He asked us a simple question, "How are you going to minister to people if you're not willing to relate to them." The rodeo is a subculture with its own way of dress. Showing up to a rodeo without a hat was like going to church without a shirt. He was right, I felt naked on my head.

The rebuke was hard to hear, especially since I wasn't even planning on being at a rodeo, ever. But that rodeo chaplain was teaching us a law. I call it the Law of the Bridge. It says, you must earn the right to speak to people by building bridges into their lives.

ALL THINGS TO ALL PEOPLE

That sounds simple enough, but this is an essential law. If a preacher doesn't follow this law, people will not listen, no matter how great a speaker they might be. Imagine you live in a rural farming community. Everyone who lives there are either farmers or grew up on farms. It's a small, tight-knit town, everyone knows everyone else. But there's nothing rural about you. You grew up a city slicker and have always lived in big cities. You are an outsider. That will come across in everything from the way you dress to the way you speak.

People might be polite to you and never tell you they feel you can't relate to them, because that's how people are. But you will see it when you preach. People sit with their arms crossed. They don't look like they are listening. How are you going to relate to them?

"WE BUILD TOO MANY WALLS AND NOT ENOUGH BRIDGES."

-Sir Isaac Newton

That's the issue we face. Maybe you're not in a farming area, maybe yours is a metropolitan city, an artsy town or a tourist destination. Maybe you've been in that area for many years and you've been with the people a lot, but you still have to work at relating to your audience. If you're brand new to an area, this can be a lot of work and take time.

This law isn't about slapping on a hat and being something you're not to trick people into thinking you're like them. It's about immersing yourself in their culture. The task is to find something your people identify with and learn more about it. If it's farming, go visit some of your people on their farms. Learn about what they do. Don't show up in a suit. Dress like them. Get yourself some boots. Show them you can work like them and help out with some chores. If they are all up at the crack of dawn every day, you do that too. Try to put yourself in their shoes and let them know you appreciate who they are and what they do. You're not some outsider who is better than them, you want to show them you respect who they are and what they do.

It's hard to identify with someone you haven't spent time with. This law is about building relationship bridges.

There is an old saying, "People don't care how much you know, until they know how much you care." The Apostle Paul said it this way, "I have become all things to all people, so that I may by every possible means save some."[7] I think that ties in perfectly with the Law of the Bridge. When you show people you are willing to identify with them you show you care. That then gives you permission to speak into their lives.

Maybe as you're reading this your thinking about your culture and you can't identify a single area that most people relate to. That's ok. The heart of this law is personal connections. It's sitting down to coffee with someone and getting in their world, cheering for that kid on the football field or sitting in someone's home and praying with them in their time of need. Some of these things we might do as our "job description" as pastors. But it's the things that fall outside the job into the arena of our personal lives that will touch people and build relationships.

I work with a team of college age students at our church. Part of what we do is travel and do ministry in different places. I train my students that when we walk into a place to do ministry, the first thing we all do is meet people. We are outsiders, so before we speak our job is to connect with people. We shake hands, take names, and chat with people, all hoping to build bridges with as many as possible before the service begins. We may never be back at that place again because we go to a lot of different places all the time, but we want to connect with people so that we have permission to speak into their lives.

The goal is getting the hands uncrossed and the

ears open so they will hear what we have to say.

LONDON BRIDGE

Bridges connect, that is their only purpose. Whether it's the lives of people or places, connection is key. There is a famous bridge you've heard of. You sang songs about it as a kid. The song goes,

> *London Bridge is falling down,*
> *Falling down, falling down*
> *London Bridge is falling down,*
> *My fair lady*

    There's debate about where the song came from but there is truth to the song. The bridge started to fall apart but not until the 1960's. It wasn't designed to handle modern traffic. Instead of repairing it the city decided to auction it off.

    Yes, that's right. You could have been the proud owner of the original London Bridge, for the right price. Most people confuse the big blue bridge with the towers for the London Bridge, but that is the Tower Bridge. The London Bridge is much less impressive, but it's still the London Bridge.

> "COMMUNICATION - THE HUMAN CONNECTION - IS THE KEY TO PERSONAL AND CAREER SUCCESS."
>
> -Paul J. Meyer

When the bridge hit the auction blocks in 1968, Robert McCulloch decided he had to have it for his town. He was the founder of Lake Havasu City, Arizona. The bridge only cost him a cool 2.4 million dollars, but it took 7 million to move it. Forget that the bridge was unnecessary. There was no water. This is Arizona we're talking about. They had built a lake, but they didn't need a bridge over it, so instead, they dug a canal. They built a concrete bridge structure on dry land near the lake, covered the bridge in the original London Bridge stones, then they dug the canal and flooded it with water.[8]

Did you catch that? They had to flood an area so the bridge would have a purpose. That's not how bridges are meant to function. They aren't supposed to be for show. The reason they put the bridge there was to drum up business for the town. The hopes were that people would want to come and see the famous London Bridge. Hopefully it doesn't fall down while they are on it! But the whole thing was for show. There was no need for a bridge.

Bridge building can't be done for show. Bridges that aren't genuine won't make connections. We must make real connections with people. You can only do that when you get involved in people's lives, not for the sake of being able to preach to them but to get to know them. You must earn permission to speak into someone's life. That takes time and effort.

Take, for example, an absent father. If he is not in the picture at home and hasn't spent time with his children, he is a father in name only. When that man shows up one day and sees his children misbehaving he will have a hard time trying to bring correction. They might be his children but that alone won't make them listen. Children won't listen to an absent parent. Why not? They haven't earned the right to speak to them. The bridges haven't been built.

Just because I'm a pastor doesn't mean people will listen to me. That might work at first. They will listen if you're new but they're trying to figure you out. If you want to continue to speak into the lives of people, you have to learn to build bridges.

Not only do we have to connect with people on a personal level we must learn to connect with them as we speak. Maybe you are in a situation where you don't know people well. You might be an evangelist or a guest speaker and you will never have the opportunity to build deep personal bridges. Shaking a hand and meeting people is a great start, but it's not the same as the relationship a pastor has with his church.

The best bridges are built by getting involved with people on a personal level. Share their struggles and their triumphs. Show them you care about them and they will want to listen to you. Put the Law of the Bridge to work in your life and ministry.

NUTS & BOLTS

- *Identify core values*

  What are the core values of the people you preach to? What kind of jobs do most people have? Is there a certain culture you live in?

- *Build bridges*

  Brainstorm ways you can build bridges into the lives of people in your church. What can you do to identify with the culture? How can you show your people that you care and are supportive of them and their families? This will be different depending on where you live and your people but here are a few ideas to get you started:

  Attend local sporting events with parents

  Meet for coffee or lunch

  Invite people over for dinner

  Start small group meetings in your church and take turns visiting each one

  Visit elderly people and help out around their house

  Or… organize a ministry team that visits elderly and helps with chores

THE LAW OF ENGAGEMENT
Effective communication demands a fully engaged audience

A joint collaboration took place in 1999 between NASA and Lockheed Martin. They worked together from two different locations to build a satellite designed to orbit Mars. The teams were composed of brilliant men and women. The teams had both worked on similar projects in the past. It should have been the perfect collaboration. The problem was the group from NASA was using standard measurements while the team from Lockheed Martin was using the metric system. The satellite was launched successfully but when the team tried to use the navigation system to steer it toward Mars, it just wouldn't work. It became space junk. The cost to NASA, $125 million, the lesson for us, priceless.[9]

Even though the project involved two talented groups of brilliant men and women, they still failed because they weren't communicating properly. They weren't speaking the same language. You've heard of the book Men are from Mars, Women are from Venus by John Gray. The premise of the book is that men and women fail to understand each other because our wiring is different. We think differently and can't understand why our spouse doesn't think like us. There are times the other person fails to communicate in a way we understand and it leaves us scratching our heads wondering what is wrong with them. There is nothing wrong. We are just built different.

This is where many sermons break down. We might have a great message but because of the way we are communicating, the message is getting lost. The difference between a good message and a great message is The Law of Engagement. To communicate effectively, we must fully engage our audience.

"FRIENDSHIP IS BORN AT THAT MOMENT WHEN ONE PERSON SAYS TO ANOTHER: 'WHAT! YOU TOO? I THOUGHT I WAS THE ONLY ONE.'"

-C.S. Lewis

If you've ever driven a car with a stick shift, you know the gears have to be engaged. If you only move the stick halfway in gear when you release the clutch you'll hear an awful grinding noise as the gears slip. You're not going anywhere like that. A transmission must be engaged fully to make any progress.

With our preaching we must learn to engage our audience fully if we want to see anything come from our messages. The Law of Engagement says, speak in a way that connects with and touches people and they will hear you.

When I was starting out I worked with youth. Over time, I learned to speak to them in a way that connected with them. Occasionally during that time I was asked to speak to the church on a Sunday morning. I remember struggling with those messages. When I spoke I felt like no one was listening. Why was I able to communicate to teenagers so well but with other age groups I felt like I was speaking a different language? It's because I was. I geared my message toward young people even though I hadn't intended it to be.

Several years later I filled in with our children's ministry for a while. I had never worked with kids and didn't have any desire to, but that's where I wound up.

When I spoke I could see the kids looking at me like I was from another planet. It took a while, but I learned how to speak to them in a way that connected with them. This may seem obvious but hold on because it's not just age levels I'm talking about. The question is how do we engage with our audience.

I do a lot of study for my messages. Sometimes I'm reading three or four commentaries on a passage. I've looked up every word in certain verses in the original Hebrew or Greek just to see if there is any additional insight. I read all my passages in several versions of the Bible. You probably do all this too. The challenge when we speak is to make what we studied relevant. The temptation is to dump everything we learned over the week on our church. If we're not careful, we can throw out so much historical background, Greek words and opinions from commentaries that our message is no longer relevant to the lives of the people we are speaking to.

We have to figure out what makes the cut. It might interest us but the guiding question for the Law of Engagement is, "Is it relevant?" If the answer is no, cut it out. This is hard for me. I might find something in my study time I think is fascinating. If I think it's so incredible the church will too, right? Maybe, or maybe not. But are you preaching to be fascinating or to speak into the lives of people in such a way as to bring them closer to God? That doesn't mean we can't bring something in occasionally we find interesting or a fun little side note, as long as those things don't distract from our message. If we are constantly bringing up all the words in Hebrew, then it's gone from interesting to boring and the audience is no longer engaged.

Bringing in things like what a commentary says about a passage or the Hebrew translation of a word is fine but they need to be used sparingly. I heard someone say once you can tell the preachers who know Hebrew or Greek versus the ones that don't. He said those who don't speak the language always want to tell what the word is. People don't care, they won't remember and they're not impressed that we looked it up, and we're probably mispronouncing it anyway. The best thing is say something like, "This word in the original language means…" You don't have to tell them the word but still use that stuff sparingly.

Be Relevant

That brings us back to our question. How do we engage our audience? To be relevant and engage people your message must address a need. How do you speak a message that addresses a need to every person in the room? You probably can't but you should try to be relevant to as many as possible. That is a huge task. Some might be employed and some aren't. There are people who are retired and those who are in school in the same room. Maybe someone is wrestling with an addiction, most people aren't. They all have different needs, how do you make your message speak into the lives of people with so much diversity in the room?

When I was working with youth the most popular messages were always the ones that had to do with dating. Everyone would perk up if I even mentioned the word. Not everyone in the room was in a dating relationship but if they weren't they wanted to be, so they would sit up on the edge of their seats listening for some tip that would help them in their relationship or would be relationship. It was relevant to where they were. It was important to them. If I took the same message to the senior citizens in our church, someone would hit me with a cane hoping to knock sense into me. They are in a different place in life. That message is no longer relevant.

I spoke a message recently about Joy. The question was, "How can we live lives filled with Joy when we're going through hard situations." Now someone who was struggling with depression will be paying a lot closer attention than someone who is not. But I tried to hit the topic in such a way as to engage everyone in the room. At certain points I would take the message to a different level with examples to make it real to each person. By the time I was done hopefully everyone in the room felt like the message was for them.

> "IT IS NOT DISTANCE THAT KEEPS PEOPLE APART BUT LACK OF COMMUNICATION."
>
> -Unknown

Finding the road to the heart of each person isn't an easy task. It takes hard work. It's easy for me to speak where I am and things that relate to me. But putting myself in someone else's shoes and thinking of what they might be facing is a much harder task. I don't know each person well. I don't know their hopes, dreams, fears and so on. But I understand what it's like to be a parent. I remember what it was like to be young. I can relate to certain things people might be facing. The key is finding what's important to as many people as possible and take that road. What is the need that most people in the room have? What can they relate to?

Selling Convertibles

We want people to have a moment when they realize this message is for them. Imagine being a car salesman. A husband and wife walk through your door with several kids in tow. You meet them and shake hands and taking them out in the lot without taking the time to get to know them. Right away you take them the two-seater convertibles with the high dollar price tag. You tell them all the perks of the car, how fast it goes from zero to sixty, the size of the engine and the high-tech navigation system. They watch speechless as you show them how to open the top and insist they take a test drive. They're too polite to walk away from you but they don't need what you're selling. You're wasting your breath. They don't care about what you have to say. You're showing them something that is not for them. It is not where they are in life. It doesn't apply to them. They're there for the mini vans. You might be able to tell I've had some bad experiences on car lots.

That's how many people are preaching. I'm not suggesting preaching the Gospel is like being a salesman but sometimes it feels like our sermons are falling on deaf ears. The problem is people aren't engaged because we're not showing them how the sermon affects their lives. What we are preaching might be good but if it doesn't affect the lives of those we are speaking to, they will tune us out.

For example, if we are preaching a salvation message to the same group of people week after week, that doesn't mean the message of salvation is wrong! But the people we are speaking to are already saved. What is our goal? Are we trying to get the same people saved repeatedly? Didn't it work the first time? Maybe those people now need to hear how to live the life God is calling them to live. That doesn't mean you don't bring in a salvation appeal each week. I try to but that is just part of my message. There might be times when I'm preaching to a group at an evangelistic crusade type of meeting and then the focus will be salvation.

D.L. Moody & The Chicago Fire

The goal is for our messages to touch the heart of

as many people as possible. So if I'm preaching about how to live a life of joy, it doesn't seem to have much to do with salvation. What I do is at the end of the message is say something like, "Today you heard how to live a life of joy. That joy only comes through a relationship with Jesus Christ. You can try to get joy in your life other ways but it won't work. Because the joy we are talking about only comes through Jesus." From there I'll give people an opportunity to come to know Jesus. That is only part of the message, an important part, but if a salvation message is not my main theme for the service I still want to work it in.

I would encourage you to always have an opportunity for people to give their lives to Jesus. I heard a story about the famous evangelist D.L. Moody. He was preaching a service in Chicago. It was the largest crowd he had ever preached to. He waited to give an altar call until the next service. He figured even more people would turn out the following week.

Moody never got to preach that message. Before he could get to the pulpit on Sunday, October 8th, 1871, the story goes, a cow tipped over a lantern in a barn and started the Great Chicago Fire. The fire burned the city for days. Hundreds died, hundreds of thousands were homeless and Moody was not able to hold the final service. He vowed from then on he would never hold a service without giving people the opportunity to surrender their lives to Christ.[10]

Every week you have different people walk through the doors of your church. There will be some who don't know the Lord and need to be offered a chance to meet Him. There are others who have been in your church for years and know the Lord but are struggling in some area. Maybe these need to hear what the Word of God says about being a godly parent, living by faith or loving their neighbor. Your job is to bring them something they need. Your job is to engage them with a message that is relevant to their lives and helps them become the people God is calling them to be.

NUTS & BOLTS

- *Find the Need*

    What needs do the people have that you will be speaking to? These usually fall into three categories:

    Spiritual – (Salvation, peace, fruit/gifts of the Spirit, witnessing, etc.) – Some issues, like sin for example, touch all three areas of a person.

    Emotional – (Depression, fear, anger, joy, love, etc.)

    Physical – (Marriage, health, finances, etc.)

- *Relate to the Need*

    Which needs does your sermon address? Make a list of the main needs you feel your sermon touches. Now go back over the message with those needs in mind. How does your message address the need? If you are preaching about marriage, how does your sermon help people have better marriages?

- *Be Relevant*

    Review your sermon for items that don't connect with your audience. Keep an eye out for anything non-essential and cut it out.

THE LAW OF THE DREAMER
Dream. Imagine what your message could look like

Do you remember the movie The Incredibles? That is one kid movie I don't mind watching with my kids. It begins with Mr. Incredible saving the day over and over. He is in a word, incredible. But everything changes when he saves a man who doesn't want to be saved. The man files a lawsuit; the result is all superheroes must go into hiding.

Years go by and we find Mr. Incredible doing nothing incredible with his life. He hates his job. His life is nothing like what he knows it could be. He has greatness inside him but he is not allowed to be great. Society has told him what he must be and how he must act and it's not incredible, it's boring.

Let me connect Mr. Incredible and our preaching. We know what a sermon should look like based on what we have seen in the past. We are taught a certain way of doing sermons. It has to look like this. It must fit into this box and have three points. It must fit into a category of expository, etc. I have nothing against three points or expository, topical or any other sort of sermons. But here's the point, in our attempt to train preachers we have inadvertently squashed creativity in the church.

> "OPTIMIST: DAY DREAMER MORE ELEGANTLY SPELLED."
>
> -Mark Twain

Some preachers are preaching the same cookie cutter sort of sermons. But this world is crying out for preachers who dream. Imagine what your sermon could look like if you did _____ (fill in the blank). Throw out the old ideas and go back to the drawing board. I'm not saying don't preach the Word of God, I'm saying be free to have creativity when you preach. Preaching and communication is an art. I've never heard of an artist that likes rules. They don't color in the lines well, they like to go outside the lines and imagine what could be.

The Law of the Dreamer says, dream and imagine what a sermon could look like with no barriers.

Barriers are the lines in a coloring book. Barriers are the treadmill when a beautiful nature trail is right outside. Barriers are like being in a swimming pool when the ocean is only a few steps away. There is freedom in dreaming. Creativity is unleashed when you are free to dream.

Be free to dream in life.

THE ULTIMATE DREAMER

God is a dreamer. Just look around at all the stuff He dreamed up. Walk through a zoo sometime. What was He thinking? He was dreaming. In fact we are still exploring His creation. In the thousands of years since man was created we have only scratched the surface. And in the last twelve months 18,000 new species have been discovered. And that is close to the average for every year. Imagine that 18,000 new species of animals and insects that have never been catalogued, were discovered last year.[11]

Let me give you a few of my favorites:

The Shape Shifting Frog

You read that right. This frog can actually change the texture of its skin. Put him on a piece of paper and he will make himself smooth to match the paper. Swap that with something bumpy like bubble wrap and his skin will match it.

The Pig Nosed Vampire Rat

It's a rat that looks like Dracula. He has huge ears and his teeth can grow over seven inches. You have to see it.

The Ninja Lantern Shark

This is my personal favorite. He has a dark body, hence the ninja name, but all of his organs glow in the dark. How cool is that?[12]

What was God thinking? He was dreaming. He could have made everything to look the same.

God creates a dog. BOOM!

"It's a dog. All dogs will be brown."

An angel walks over and admires the dog, "Wow nice dog, but what about some other colors? Maybe someone would like a white one."

"Nope. Only brown. All dogs will be brown."

God's not boring, so your sermon shouldn't be either. Be free to dream and imagine. There's no pressure here to be like anyone else or make your sermon like someone else's. Communicate the Word of God however you like. If you want to use a crazy illustration, go for it. The point is dream. Ask questions. Use the God given creativity you have.

STOP DREAMING, START DYING

Look what it says in Joel 2:28,

After this

I will pour out My Spirit on all humanity;

then your sons and your daughters will prophesy,

your old men will have dreams,

and your young men will see visions.

I've wondered about that verse. Why does it say old men will dream but young men will have visions? I realize the point is, God is showing He is including every demographic in this outpouring. But I was thinking about old men and dreaming. Most old men don't dream. I don't mean literally, but dreaming has do with the future. You dream about what your life will be like when you're young. When you're dating a girl you dream about the future together. When you have children you dream about what they will become. But most old men don't dream. They reach a stage where the dreaming stops.

But God says in the last days old men will dream. It doesn't matter how old or young you are, you were made to dream. Dream about what church could look like. Dream about what your sermons could look like. When you stop dreaming you start dying.

We have a lot of traditions in the church. Preaching hasn't changed much in hundreds of years. There is nothing wrong with that but just because we've done it the same way for hundreds of years doesn't make it the only way. Jesus was a preacher. In fact that was the first thing He read when He began His ministry. He stood up in a synagogue and took the scroll of Isaiah and read:

The Spirit of the Lord is on Me, because He has anointed Me to preach good news to the poor. (Luke 4:18)

He had an anointing to preach. He was a preacher. But His preaching looks almost nothing like ours. Does that make our preaching bad? No, it means it's different. Different is good, but most of us aren't different from one another, we all sound the same. Be different, be unique.

Preach the way God is calling you to preach.

"ALL MEN DREAM; BUT NOT EQUALLY. THOSE WHO DREAM BY NIGHT IN THE DUSTY RECESSES OF THEIR MINDS WAKE IN THE DAY TO FIND THAT IT WAS VANITY: BUT THE DREAMERS OF THE DAY ARE DANGEROUS MEN, FOR THEY MAY ACT THEIR DREAMS WITH OPEN EYES, TO MAKE IT POSSIBLE."
-T.E. Lawrence

Our society doesn't think this way. We don't encourage dreaming in Western culture. In fact when you go to school they'll try to medicate you if you're dreaming too much. They want you to look and sound like everyone else so you can fit in to society. But that's not how God created us. We wind up like Mr. Incredible. We know we were made for more. I think there are a lot of frustrated preachers out there. Maybe they can't put their finger on what is frustrating them but in the back of their minds they keep thinking, "This can't be all there is."

If that's you today, guess what, there's more. Just like any good infomercial. There's more. There is a deeper dreaming God is calling you to.

One of my favorite Scriptures is I Corinthians 2:9-10,

> But as it is written: What eye did not see and ear did not hear, and what never entered the

human mind-- God prepared this for those who love Him. Now God has revealed these things to us by the Spirit, for the Spirit searches everything, even the depths of God.

It sounds a lot like dreaming. Some people take this verse only in reference to what God has prepared in heaven for us. Now heaven will be good and that verse certainly fits the description of heaven, but I don't think that's the only application. It's talking about now. God has prepared things for you now in this life and in heaven.

God desires to reveal things to you that you've never seen before. We've never heard it. It's never entered our minds. But God has prepared it for us! He goes on to say God has revealed these things to us by His Spirit. That means we should not be ignorant of the good things God has planned for us. We are supposed to be coworkers with Him. I need to get together with God and dreaming. God wants to reveal things to us. Things we can't think up on our own. Things that will blow your mind. That's the kind of God He is. He is a mind-blowing God.

Look at what Jesus says in John 5:19-20

Then Jesus replied, "I assure you: The Son is not able to do anything on His own, but only what He sees the Father doing. For whatever the Father does, the Son also does these things in the same way. For the Father loves the Son and shows Him everything He is doing, and He will show Him greater works than these so that you will be amazed.

Did you catch that? Jesus would be doing greater works from the Father. But did you see why? What was the reason He told them? So they would be amazed. That word amazed translates, "astonished out of one's senses."

That sounds a lot like mind blowing to me. He wants to blow our minds with what He has prepared for us. But you can't see it with your natural senses. It's nothing you've ever seen or heard. It's beyond anything that's entered your mind. God has things in store for your life and your ministry that you can only access by His Spirit. Start dreaming with Him.

When you are dreaming together with God people will look at what you've done and say, "Where on earth did you come up with that? I've never seen anything like it before."

And you can say, "I didn't get it from anywhere on earth. It came straight from the Spirit of God."

We're called to live that kind of life and that should come through when we preach. I heard someone say, "Everything is created twice." First it's created in your mind or imagination, the place where you dream. If you don't dream it you won't do it. Put the Law of the Dreamer to work in your life and in your sermon and see what God will do.

NUTS & BOLTS

- *Dream*

    Spend some time this week thinking about your sermons. If possible schedule someone else to preach so you have time to focus on "dreaming."

    Ask yourself some questions:

    How can you make your sermon more exciting, creative, or engaging?

    What are some things you would like to change about your sermons?

    What elements would you add if you had the resources?

- *Make it happen*

    Now that you've been dreaming what do you need to do in order to make it a reality? Maybe you can scale down your idea to make it fit where you are at the moment and keep the big version as a goal.

    Do you need to share the vision? If it's a big enough dream get others in on the idea. If you want to incorporate a drama team to work on skits for your messages you are going to need some people. Share the vision and get others to come along with you.

THE LAW OF THE LISTENER
You will become what you consistently listen to

    For centuries if someone wanted to learn a trade they needed to find a teacher to train them. If they wanted to learn carpentry, they needed to find a master carpenter to teach them wood working skills. A young apprentice might sit in a blacksmith shop for endless hours watching the blacksmith, cleaning the shop, fetching water, all the while learning the trade of a smith.

    We don't use the word apprentice much anymore, but they are still around. Sometimes we call them by different names, like interns. We tend to look down on an intern in society. We pity the poor guy who would actually work for little or no pay. With the exception of someone working in a trade we tend to think on-the-job training is unnecessary. Maybe you spent time as an intern as part of a college requirement but I would guess that most people go to school and launch out into the world with little or no practical training. The intern on the other hand is learning in a hands on environment. Maybe he is just interning in an office setting where he is running for coffee and cleaning up the break room, but he is learning how to work in an environment where he hopes to spend his future. Being an intern is an incredible way to learn a business, trade or craft.

Preaching is no different. Most preachers learn in a classroom how to put together a sermon or they read books like this one (good for you by the way!) They might preach to their classmates once or twice. Then they find themselves thrust into a church to practice preaching on the poor people while they figure it out. What they need is the Law of the Listener. Without this law implemented a preacher will never grow to become all they can be.

"WHEN PEOPLE TALK, LISTEN COMPLETELY. MOST PEOPLE NEVER LISTEN."
-Ernest Hemingway

The Law of the Listener could also be called the Law of the Apprentice, the idea is the same. The Law of the Listener says, listen to and learning from great preachers regularly and you will become like what you consistently listen to. It doesn't matter if you've been preaching for a year or fifty years. One of the greatest ways to learn is to listen to others. Find great preachers and listen to a couple of them a week. These men and women of God will become your mentors and your teachers. The goal of the Law of the Listener is to become an apprentice who listens well.

I know this sounds like a contradiction to the previous law, The Law of the Dreamer, where I told you to dream and don't try to make your sermon a typical cookie cutter message. However, these laws can work together. In the Law of the Listener you are cultivating a practice of listening to great communicators. But you are not trying to copy them or replicate their style or structure. You are listening to learn how to communicate well. Your message is still unique. You have dreamed and come up with a creative message or a creative approach. This is all about learning and developing communication skills.

This has become easier with the invention of podcast that most of us can access right from our phones. There are so many choices out there so make sure you find someone who has been around for a while and knows how to preach. Turn them on when you're in the car or the gym and listen to not only what they are saying but also how they are saying it. You are not trying to copy anyone. I'm not encouraging you to become a copycat preacher. You are not listening to steal sermons or preaching styles. Please, be yourself. You are listening to learn how to preach better. You may hear something that inspires a message in you that's great! A certain scripture someone uses, or an illustration has inspired me. It's ok to use something you hear as long as you credit the person. But the point is, we become better as we listen to others.

We all have room for improvement. But if we never hear great preaching, we don't know what it sounds like. Maybe you go to a conference occasionally and hear great preaching so you think that's good enough. Nope. You need to hear it regularly. I would suggest once a week. Maybe you grew up in an amazing church with a world-class preacher so you think this doesn't apply to you. Nope. You need to be exposed to more than just one great preacher and you need it on a recurring basis.

REFRIGERATOR ART

This may sound like a strange law but if you want to move from being a good preacher to a great preacher, you need to follow this. My kids love arts and crafts. They are constantly doing crafts all over our house. There are paintings of unicorns hanging on my walls. All of my Tupperware is filled with slime made of glue and laundry detergent. In fact, I have no glue or laundry detergent left in my house. The other day I sat down with them and colored a picture using crayons and a coloring book. I understand why there are adult coloring books. You can get lost in the monotony of scribbling on a page. When I finished I went looking for some magnets to hang it on the fridge. Why not? It's just as good as my kids art.

Here's my point. If my only exposure to art is my kids coloring and painting, I can sit down and think I am a terrific artist. I step back and look at my coloring of a bear and a rainbow and realize all of my color is inside the lines. My crayon strokes are even and in the same direction. The realization hits me, I might be the greatest artist in the room. I decide to frame my art and donate it to an art museum. While I am waiting for my appointment with the curator, I decide to take a stroll and look at the art. As I walk down the halls I'm awestruck, looking from wall to wall at the work of masters. My coloring doesn't seem so fantastic anymore.

That is enough for most of us to never want to visit the work of masters. We know that we will wind up comparing ourselves to them and we will come up short. No one ever wins in the comparison game. This isn't about comparison. It might intimidate or even humble us at first to listen to some great preaching, but it's necessary to become the best we can be. It's not about comparison but it's all about study. If I go to the museum to study the work and learn what I can, my work will improve. My craft will come up to another level.

When you listen to someone else preach you're not trying to break apart their sermon in a critical way you are listening to learn. Pay attention to how they communicate. What do they do to engage the audience? How are they opening their message? What about it makes you want to keep listening? After the message think about the sermon. Was there anything you can apply to your own preaching? Again you are not trying to be a photocopy of another preacher but you are trying to learn from their methods. Learn from their experience.

If you're listening to a preacher at a huge church, keep in mind they have a staff of people and will sometimes collaborate with multiple people as they put together a message. Their team will do research for them, finding excellent illustrations and so on. They also might have an executive pastor who runs the day-to-day operations of the church so the pastor you're listening to can focus on preaching. So don't be intimidated when you hear an outstanding message. But also don't use excuses for not becoming better yourself. You can preach as good a sermon as anyone else out there. You have the same Spirit that raised Christ from the dead living in you. He is with you and is anointing you. So study and do your best and He will work through you.

I realized this law after I had been preaching for about a decade. I hadn't had much exposure to other preachers except for guys who visited our church or one of our staff preaching. Occasionally I saw someone on TV or got a hold of a CD but that was about it. One day I discovered a thing called podcast on my newfangled cell phone. I was hooked. At the time my commute to work was about twenty minutes so I could listen to an entire sermon on my round-trip commute every day. It didn't register how much of an impact it was having on me until one day I was preaching and in the middle of my sermon I almost had to stop and say, "Wow, where did all that come from?" I had been hearing so much good preaching that I was starting to preach better. I wasn't copying anyone, but I realized that I was becoming like what I was listening to. The discipline of listening was making me a better preacher and I could notice a difference. If you'll listen to great preaching, you will not be able to help it, you will preach better.

FAITH COMES BY HEARING

Another reason for this law, beyond learning how to be a better preacher, is to encourage you. Let's be honest, if the only preaching you hear during the week is you, you need more. It's encouraging to hear someone else preaching. They might even preach the same thing as you, but it's different when you hear it from someone else. The more you hear the word of God the more the word of God will come out of you when you need it. Faith comes by hearing the Word and we need to be hearing more. There are some excellent preachers out there who have been encouraging in my walk with the Lord. Since I started listening to preaching regularly I have grown in my own life.

"THE BIGGEST COMMUNICATION PROBLEM IS WE DO NOT LISTEN TO UNDERSTAND. WE LISTEN TO REPLY."
-Unknown

You understand this idea why it's so beneficial to be hearing the Word regularly. You might even have your own podcast and encourage your church to listen. They need it but so do you. You need to be a listener. It's not a good idea to skip any of the laws. They are laws for a reason. We ignore the law at our own risk. The speed limit sign is there for a reason. All of the laws work together to help you form a sermon that will change lives and impact people for the Kingdom of God. But there are laws we might call Cardinal Laws. Like the Law of the Boiler or the Law of Direction. The Law of the Listener is right up there. Without it you won't have the exposure to great preaching you need to become a great preacher yourself. But even more important without it your own spiritual development will be lacking. This law transcends your preaching and moves into a personal area. As you listen and study, these men and women of God you will you be changed.

Being a pastor can be a depressing job. Don't get me wrong, most of the time I find it wonderful and fulfilling. But there are moments when you might wonder, "Why am I doing this?" "Why do I keep preaching and nothing happens?" In these moments it's important to remember you are in a spiritual battle. There is a real enemy who wants to destroy you, your family and everything you touch. The only way you can keep going in these times is if you are grounded in the Word of God. He is your source and your strength. We talk more about this in a later chapter but the Law of the Listener is one of the keys to standing firm in hard times. When you are consistently listening to people preaching the Word of God, you will find encouragement to keep going. Time and again I have turned on a podcast only to hear exactly what I needed at that moment.

I believe you will be encouraged and refreshed while learning to become a better communicator as you practice the Law of the Listener in your life.

NUTS & BOLTS

- *Set it up*

    If you've never listened to podcasts take some time and set this up. You can do it across most devices.

    Search for podcasts from several different preachers. The goal here is to go for variety and not get stuck on just one person, as good as they might be.

- *Find a listening time*

    Decide when your listening time is going to be. It needs to be a consistent time that you have each week. If you have a long commute, this is a perfect time. My commute is shorter lately so I use my workout time.

- *Take notes*

    Keep a notepad handy and jot down ideas as you listen. You are going to start picking out key elements each person uses as they communicate. Its important to write these down so you can reinforce the ideas you learn. You may also get some ideas for messages.

THE LAW OF THE SPEAR
Every good message must have a point, if not it will be dull and useless

I was young and just starting out as a youth pastor in a small church when I learned The Law of the Spear. I remember we had a visiting preacher that day. He was exciting. He spoke with an energy that electrified the room. His message was filled with passion but I was wondering where he was going. That's when the message ended, without warning. I stood up to leave and thought, "What was the point?"

Now please don't misunderstand me, I'm not a critical person and I'm not encouraging us to be critical of others when they preach. I know I don't want that when I preach. But as a young man I realized there has to be a point, or else what's the point?

It's like going to a movie with no plot! I remember seeing some of those. If you can make it through the whole movie, you leave thinking, "What a waste of time?" Have you ever left a movie and said, "There's two hours I'll never get back." None of us want anyone to leave our sermon saying the same thing. The point is, you must have a point.

Imagine getting on an airplane without a destination in mind. That would be interesting. The pilot would come on the intercom, "Attention ladies and gentlemen, today we'll be cruising at thirty-five thousand feet for, well, we'll just have to see how long this fuel holds up. I think maybe I'll steer this bird north for a while then make a big swing west, or maybe east. You know what I think I'll go south instead. Thank you for choosing, Wandering Airlines."

When you get short on fuel, the pilot will land, as long as there is land in sight, and an airport. How do you pack for that kind of trip?

Would you like to buy a ticket on Wandering Air? I know there might be some out there who would like to try that. But let's be honest, it might be ok once or even twice, but most of the time we travel we like to have a destination in mind.

Now would you like to hear a sermon like that? Well maybe it would be all right occasionally, just strap your belt on and let's see where this bird lands, kind of sermon. But not every week!

Your sermon is like a spear. You are preaching the Word of God directed at the heart of each person in the room. But if your spear doesn't have a point, it's just a stick. Try fishing with a dull hook, the fish will just spit it out. Unless you learn The Law of the Spear that is exactly what people will do with your sermon. Spit it out. The message won't get to their heart because they will not understand what you are trying to say. You can be an entertaining, dynamic, charismatic speaker but if you don't have a point, forget about it!

"IT'S BETTER TO SAY NOTHING THAN SPEND 1000 WORDS OR AN HOUR SPEECH SAYING NOTHING. GET TO THE POINT - FAST."

-Richard Branson

This is the most important part of developing your sermon. It's the reason you're speaking. It's the one thing you want people to remember when they leave.

I know what you're thinking. You have a lot of points you want to drive home in every message. Maybe. But you need to have ONE main idea or theme. I'm not saying keep your sermon shallow. Just stick to one main idea. That is your point, you're not wielding a trident it's a spear. There is room for depth, it's just a focused depth. If you find yourself creating multiple themes, BOOM! You have yourself a sermon series. So often preachers want to preach an entire series every single week. Save something for next time.

Some people get hung up on having three points. Other people insist you should only have one. I've heard sermons with a dozen points before. That was a workout, both for the preacher and for me. But honestly, you can have as many or as few points as you like but you should have only one theme. You need to be able to explain your message in just a few words.

DEVELOP THE PLOT

Look at the movie example. A good movie has a story and a plot. It might have a car chase but that doesn't mean it has to be a movie about. It might feature a character playing the role of the President but that doesn't mean it's a political movie. Even with different characters and a storyline that has action taking place around the globe there is one main theme.

Speaking of cars, I recently re-watched the movie Cars, with my kids. I know what you're thinking: this guy watches a lot of kid movies. But it kind of goes with the territory of having kids. If you've been around kids anytime in the last decade you've probably seen it or at least know what it's about. It's about cars, right? No. It has cars in the movie, but it's not about cars.

In the movie the character Lightning McQueen is a race car. Lightning is the newest, fastest and the best race car out there. He wants to win. That's all he cares about. People, I mean cars, aren't important to him. There is no one important in Lightning's life except for Lightning. He is cocky and arrogant and as a result no one wants to work with him.

Stay with me. He falls off his truck and winds up in jail in a small town. There he learns about friendship and the need to have other people in his life. It's not a movie about cars. You wouldn't get so emotional watching a flick about cartoon cars. (I only cried a little). It's emotional because it's about friendship.

You see where this is going. There is one theme for an entire movie. You need one theme. Find your theme get it down to a few words or less and drive it home. Repeat it again, and again until people will hear it in their sleep.

Now please understand, this may take time to reprogram your sermon writing habits. It takes work to narrow your thoughts. Writing a sermon is hard work. It's demanding and relentless. As soon as you finish one you're off on the next one. This is where it becomes helpful to be purposefully narrow with your topic. When you want to jump into another point but you feel it doesn't tie in closely enough, save it for a sermon series or a part two.

This applies to every type of sermon. Some preachers love expository sermons. They take a huge passage and preach on it. I think those can be great messages. But even in a large portion of Scripture you need to find ONE central theme. If you can't identify what your sermon is about in a few words, no one else will be able to either. Remember you don't want to take people for a ride on Wandering Air week after week.

I preached a sermon recently titled, Get to Work, based on Romans 8:28

> *And we know [with great confidence] that God [who is deeply concerned about us] causes all things to work together [as a plan] for good for those who love God, to those who are called according to His plan and purpose.* (AMP)

In the sermon I focused on the story of Joseph. I spoke about his attitude in the face of adversity. But everything came back to this one point: everything was working for good in Joseph's life. It's encouraging to hear God had a plan for Joseph so I know He has a plan for me. God worked everything for Joseph so He's working everything for me.

I don't believe God caused the bad things that happened to Joseph but God used it all for good. My theme was: Get to Work. The message was to encourage that no matter what you might be going through God will make that thing get to work for you. The devil might have sent it to destroy you but God is making it work for you. I kept coming back to those three words, Get to Work.

GETTING TO THE POINT

Let me take you through some steps I use to help me get to my point. After praying I think about my topic. Sometimes I have a strong impression that the Lord wants me to go a certain direction. Sometimes I don't. If I'm not sure what to preach about, I will look through my Bible and what I've been reading. I think about what the Lord has been speaking to me through what I've been reading. I look through any notes I've made. Is there something there that might make a good message?

If I think I've found something I pray some more and ask the Lord. Maybe I outline what the sermon would look like. Now if I feel comfortable with it I will run with that.

Before I even start writing the message I read and research. First, I'll go through the chapter or if it's in a smaller book of the Bible, I'll read the whole book and make sure I have a good grasp of the entire subject. Next I read some commentaries about the passage and look up keywords in the text for additional insight. I won't bother to bring it up when I preach unless there is something worth mentioning. I'm not trying to dazzle anyone with my grasp of Hebrew or Greek. They won't be impressed!

I've listed some of my favorite resources at the end of the book. (see Appendix A)

The point in all this is so you will know your topic well. As I'm preaching I use notes, but I want to be familiar with my topic so that if I get lost or want to take a side trail, I can do it.

After I'm familiar with my point, I start building my message. I skip the introduction and go straight for the main points unless something is jumping out at me. I don't get too worried about how many points I have. I don't want too many because I don't want to preach for two hours, but I'm not concerned with having three points. As long as you have a point you're doing good.

ASKING THE RIGHT QUESTION

Your sermon should answer a question. I'm sure you know this but we need to stop and ask ourselves what is the question. We are addressing a need in the lives of people. What is the need? What is the question my sermon is answering? If I don't know the question, I don't really know what my message is about.

> "IF I HAD AN HOUR TO SOLVE A PROBLEM AND MY LIFE DEPENDED ON IT, I WOULD USE THE FIRST 55 MINUTES DETERMINING THE PROPER QUESTIONS TO ASK."
>
> -Albert Einstein

As you preach your sermon needs to answer the question. Every point, every illustration, every Scripture is sharpening your spear, bringing you closer and closer to your point. If you find yourself working on part of your message that doesn't fit with the question, dump it. Again to have a point you need to be clear. You don't want to be known as the preacher who always takes the rabbit trails. Find the main path and stick to it.

So get to the point. Put the Law of the Spear to work in your messages and let them fly. The sharper they are the better they will stick.

NUTS & BOLTS

- *Ask the question*

    As you begin to prepare for your message this week ask yourself, what is the question of my sermon? In the Law of Engagement you found the need, how does your sermon address that need? Write the question down. Refer to that question often as you work through the process of writing.

- *Rehearse the question*

    After you're done writing go over your sermon with the question written in front of you. Is your sermon sticking to the question? If it's going off somewhere take those notes out and set them aside (maybe you have the beginning of a series.) Stick to the question.

- *Stick to the point*

    Now you have a sharp spear. Your job is to stick to the point. It's tempting to run off the trail when a thought pops in your head, don't do it.

THE LAW OF CHEWING THE CUD
Find your message early and chew on it

I can still remember a field trip our class took when I was in elementary school. It stands out as one of the strangest experiences of my childhood. We went to a farm. (I lived in Ohio, so this was a normal field trip for us.) I don't remember anything else about the trip except for this one cow. This sad old cow had a problem and had to have her stomach cut open. Instead of stitching her back up someone came up with the idea of putting a rubber gasket on her. The gasket stayed closed and kept things out, but if you wanted to, you could put your hand through the gasket and pull stuff out of her stomach. Which, of course, led to groups of school children taking field trips to put their hands inside this poor cows belly.

When it was my turn, I put on one of those rubber gloves and pushed my hand through the hard rubber. Steam poured out from the guts of the cow into the cold barn. It smelled like a lawnmower had just thrown up. I reached down inside the animal and my hands touched the contents of the stomach. It was like dipping your finger in a hot tub full of slime and grass. It was a great morning for everyone. The farmer asked me to pull out some hot slime and see what it was. This seemed like a good idea so I grabbed a handful and pulled it out. It was the nastiest glob of chewed up grass you can imagine.

With my hands full of half digested straw and grass the farmer explained that a cow will eat her food, digest it a while, then regurgitate it back into her mouth to chew it some more. I felt like regurgitating my breakfast.

But cows will do this. When something is too big for them to digest at once they spit it up and chew it again. It's called chewing the cud. And that brings us to The Law of Chewing the Cud. This law says, Find your message early and chew on it for a while.

OWN THE MESSAGE

This law requires you to find a message early. I realize it might not be possible 100% of the time. There might be times when you feel the Lord pulling you a different direction the night before, or even as you walk up to the pulpit. There may be those occasions when you are called to preach somewhere last minute and you don't have the time to find a message early. But these are the exceptions not the rule. You can't preach a message you don't own. If you do you will struggle through it. What I mean by that is when you haven't processed the message in your own heart it may come across flat. It won't have the depth it should because you aren't connected to it.

When you have the time to discover a topic and wander around inside it, you'll find the message gets to be a part of you. As it bounces around in your heart for a day or two parts of the sermon will become obvious. When the sermon gets inside you like that, you are no longer sharing a bunch of thoughts you've written down, you're speaking from your heart. It's a lot easier to speak from your heart, instead of just giving a speech you are preaching from the fire that's been stirred inside you.

"YOU CAN'T PREACH A MESSAGE YOU DON'T OWN."

Chewing on a message for several days gives you time to explore all the possibilities of where this thing might go. You can dive into every nook and cranny of the topic. Some elements of the sermon might pop up at you after a couple days of chewing that you didn't even think about on day one. The chewing process allows you to connect to the message and that will come across as you share it.

LEARNING TO SPIT

The other thing chewing a message will let you do is spit it out if you need to. When you have time you can do this, but when you're starting the message the night before you can't. You need to have time to spit because there are times as you start down the path of creating and writing the sermon when you will feel it isn't going where you want. Sometimes you can save it with some redirection but there are times when it needs to be spit out. Don't worry what your mother told you, spitting is part of the process. It's going to happen. You can tuck those notes you've made so far away for future use on some other message, perhaps, but you need to know when it's time to move on.

This might feel frustrating because you have to move back to square one but sometimes it's easier to start over than keep working on a sermon that's broken. It's like a car you keep fixing. Have you ever spent more on repairing a car than the car is worth? I have. I wish I had sold that thing before doing the repairs because a year later I had to sell it for less than my repairs cost me. That's frustrating. It's also frustrating working on a sermon and realizing it's not going to work for me. It's better to spit it out early, if I can see it won't work. This takes practice. Sometimes a sermon is good and you can use it you just have to know how to make it work.

Maybe you have implemented the Law of Chewing the Cud on your own, but if you haven't let me emphasize how important this is. When you do this, you will realize a difference immediately as you preach. Instead of feeling stuck to your notes and having to keep checking to see what comes next you'll find the message just flowing out of you. If you wanted to, you could walk away from your notes entirely and preach. That doesn't mean you've memorized your message, and it doesn't mean you wouldn't miss things. But you have the important pieces digested.

> "OPEN UP MY UNDERSTANDING TO THE WAYS OF YOUR WISDOM AND I WILL MEDITATE DEEPLY ON YOUR SPLENDOR AND YOUR WONDERS."
>
> -Psalm 119:27

EATING THE WHALE

So how do we do this? How do we chew the cud? You might wonder how there could be time for that. If you only have a week to get ready how do you have time to chew on a sermon? Let me walk you through the process.

When I'm preparing a sermon, I set time aside early in the week to find my topic. I get alone in a room with my Bible and a notepad and spend time in prayer. I want to know where God wants me to go. Sometimes before I come in I already have several notes from the previous week. Maybe as I was praying or reading my Bible the Lord spoke to me, or something jumped off the page at me and I made a note. I mentioned a prayer journal in the first chapter but you need to get another journal for your preaching. You can use notes on your phone or tablet but you need somewhere you can jot down all those great ideas that come to you. Keep the journal with you during your prayer and study times.

So I pray, I review my notes and wait until I have an idea where I should go with the message. Sometimes it might take a few minutes, sometimes an hour or more. I'm not trying to walk out of the room with a full sermon, just a passage of Scripture and an idea where it's going. That is all I'm looking for. I'm not trying to write this thing in one shot because I know if I do I will rewrite it several times. My goal is to get an idea, a thought that will turn into a sermon.

I jot this thought down on a notepad and keep it on my desk for a day or two. It's not hanging over my head. It's a reminder of where I'm going. Every time I see it, I think about the sermon and things take shape. Throughout my day thoughts come to me about my sermon, sometimes I'll find myself preaching the message while I'm driving or in the shower and think, "That's good. I need to remember that." Then I'll jot those things down on my notepad. In a couple days I have a rough outline of what my sermon should look like. I'm chewing my cud.

It's a big task to prepare a sermon and it can feel overwhelming. Kind of like a cow trying to digest something too big for her. It needs to be broken down more. So break your sermon down. Even just an hour early in the week will help you break it down, getting it into bite size pieces. Then revisit it later.

I find it works like this for me. If I find a message, get a couple thoughts together and walk away, when I revisit the message in couple days I realize I've been processing it even if I haven't purposely sat down to work on it. My mind and my spirit have been pouring over the Word while I go about other things. Even while I'm sleeping! I have woken up in the middle of the night and had part of my sermon playing through my head.

The next time I sit down to work on my message it is so much easier because I've been processing it. Once I'm done, I have a message that has come from inside me. I'm connected to it. It can be a daunting task to write a sermon. Someone who has never had to do it would not understand how much work is involved. Like any big project it's good to break it down into bite size pieces. There is a great poem by Shel Silverstein about a little girl who wanted to eat a whale. It goes like this:

> *Have you heard of tiny Melinda Mae,*
>
> *Who ate a monstrous whale?*
>
> *She thought she could,*
>
> *She said she would,*
>
> *So she started right in at the tail.*
>
> *And everyone said, "You're much to small,"*
>
> *But that didn't bother Melinda at all,*
>
> *She took little bites and chewed very slow,*
>
> *Just like a good girl should…*
>
> *…And in eighty-nine years she ate that whale*
>
> *Because she said she would!*[13]

Writing a sermon is a little like eating a whale. The best way to do it is one bite at a time. Not only will you save yourself a headache from trying to tackle it all at once but going through the process will help you connect to the message. As you implement the Law of Chewing the Cud, you will find the message flows out of you as you speak and people will connect with the Word of God in a real way.

NUTS & BOLTS

- *Journal*

    Get a dedicated journal for sermon notes, preferably something you can carry with you. This could be digital but if you like using a physical book than use that. The point here is to find something that works for you and actually use it. Have this handy all the time.

- *Plan*

    Start planning out your message by Monday or Tuesday this week. This doesn't need to be a full-blown sermon writing time. Just take an hour and start thinking about your sermon.

    Choose your passage of Scripture. Find a topic. Pick your theme. If you're not preaching this week get started on the next message.

- *Chew*

    Review what you have so far for a couple of days and make some notes. Leave your sermon on your desk, or someplace where you will see it often. Read it over and make any notes that come to you as you're chewing on it.

    Jot down additional Scriptures, illustration ideas, or any thoughts that further develop your theme.

- *Finish*

    Sit down and polish off your sermon. Finish writing your sermon by Friday. That will give you time to make any changes and chew on the finished product a little more before you preach on Sunday.

THE LAW OF THE TEE OFF
If you want to people to listen, start well

When the game of golf was being introduced to the United States a Scottish man was asked to demonstrate for President Ulysses Grant. The man showed the President the tee and stuck it in the ground. He showed him the ball and carefully placed it on the tee. Then the man took out his club and addressed the ball. He took a powerful swing and sent dirt flying all over the President's beard. There the ball sat, still on the tee. The man swung again and missed.

After six attempts the President said, "There seems to be a fair amount of exercise in this game, but I fail to see the purpose of the ball."[14]

You've heard the saying, "You never get a second chance to make a first impression." The same is true for preaching. You never get a second chance to capture your audience's attention. I heard someone once say if you don't capture their attention in the first five minutes, then you've lost them for the rest of the message. You may have what you think is a killer message. But if you can't get anyone to listen, it will not be effective. You're just a tree falling in the forest with no one around. Did anyone hear that? Why do I feel like I'm preaching to myself? Maybe you lost them.

It may sound immature or unspiritual that we have to come up with something to make people want to listen. Aren't they in church? Didn't they come to hear the Word of God? The truth is you might have some people listening to you no matter what. Some people are more disciplined listeners and have taught themselves to pay attention. These are your note takers. They're writing down every reference and jotting down as much of your sermon as they can. But let's be honest, how many of those do you have in the room each Sunday? And even those guys might only look engaged. How do you know if they're doodling or making a grocery list?

Let's be polite and assume your note takers are hanging on every word, for the rest of the group you need to give them a reason to listen. The way you start your message is the most important part of your sermon, hands down. Why should they care? Why should they listen? How you tee off makes all the difference.

Now I'm not a golfer but I know something about golf. If you tee off well you put yourself in a good position for the next couple of shots. You want to be as close to the pin as possible and hopefully in the center of the fairway. From there it should just be a shot or two to the green. If you tee off poorly and wind up in the rough, behind some trees, far away from the green, you have an uphill battle.

You find yourself trying to recover. This is the part of the game that brings out the emotion in people. This is where clubs are thrown and four letter words are shouted, golf is a four letter word by the way.

The way you tee off can leave you feeling excited for the rest of the hole or frustrated and ready to quit. It's the same for your sermon. If you can nail the tee off you're set up for the rest of the message. It's just a couple of chip shots from there to the conclusion.

"DO YOU SUPPOSE I COULD BUY BACK MY INTRODUCTION TO YOU?"

-Groucho Marx

The Law of the Tee Off says: start well, take a hold of the attention of the people as you begin and they are more likely to listen to the rest of your message.

START WITH THE ACTION

Think about a good action movie (the emphasis is on the word good). They don't start out slow. If they begin with all the background to the story, filling you in on all the character details, why the bad guy became the bad guy, and on and on, you'd be bored to death before any action took place. No, a good action movie starts with ACTION. There is an explosion, a gunfight, a car chase, something like that. They'll give you the details later and you're fine with it.

Start your sermon like that. With a bang.

I know, it sounds like a lot of work. It is. Putting together your introduction might be the hardest part of your message. But you can't skip this step. This is the reason people will continue listening.

"IF YOU START WITH A BANG, YOU WON'T END WITH A WHIMPER."

-T.S. Elliot

Go listen to someone give a speech sometime. Notice how the person begins. If they're good, they will grab your attention. Sales people especially know this because if they don't get your attention they don't feed their family. They want to start out and grab your attention and try to hold it until they sell you whatever it is they have.

Now think about your sermon. Are you grabbing attention from the beginning or are you more like the golfer who can't hit the ball? You need a great tee off.

THE BEST MEDICINE

You need to do what fits you and your specific message. I don't always start the same way. I try to use humor as I begin. That doesn't mean I always use humor but sometimes I do. I find people let the guards down when they laugh.

Now I heard a preacher criticize this idea once. He

thought preachers who use humor aren't really preachers, they are just clowns and have no place in the pulpit. That's pretty strong and I seriously disagree. Even the Bible says, "A joyful heart is good medicine."[15] Some people need to laugh, everyone needs to laugh but some people really need it. If some preachers laughed more, they wouldn't have such sour expressions on their faces all the time. I know we have a serious business. I realize there are lost people going to hell. But if we show them that being a Christian means you can be full of joy, well I don't think that's a bad thing.

I'm not saying you should try to make your entire message one big comedy act. There is a time to be more serious. But I don't think it's a bad thing to bring in some humor now and then. I enjoy it and I think the people who listen to our sermons do too. But be yourself. If humor doesn't come natural for you, please use something else. Don't try to be something you're not. Again, it's not a comedy act so don't feel like you have to use that. Use a gripping story. Use a video clip. Have your youth group put together a skit. You can even bring someone up and have them share a testimony.

Experiment and find something that will fit well with your message. Whatever I use for my introduction I always want it to have a point. I don't want to bring in a joke just to tell a joke. There needs to be a purpose behind it. It needs to connect. I want my introduction pointing at my ending. The laser is already engaged from the moment I walk on the stage.

Whatever you do, be creative. I remember seeing a guy preach once in Army fatigues. He wasn't in the army, it was for his illustration. At one point this guy took out a pack of firecrackers and lit them inside a trashcan. It was memorable.

Don't do something like that every week or you'll kill yourself... and the church might think you're crazy. But we need to use things that help people listen well.

FINDING GOLD

I prepare my intro last because it's the hardest part and I want it all to tie together. I might spend as much time finding a good intro as I do writing a majority of my sermon unless I already have my intro in hand. A lot of times when I come across something and I think, that would be perfect for an illustration, I'll make a note.

"THE BEGINNING IS THE MOST IMPORTANT PART OF THE WORK."

-Plato

I know of one guy who keeps a binder of illustrations. When he comes across an article or a story he thinks would be a good illustration he makes a copy and sticks it in the binder. He keeps it all organized by topic. I'm not at that organization level but it would make my life much easier. So be on the lookout for good illustrations. Even if it doesn't fit for your message this time, if it's good file it away.

I've tried to get into a habit of reading a variety of books. I've never been into biographies but I read a couple lately and loved the stories. As I read I'm always on the lookout for things that will make a good illustration. I recently read a biography on John Wayne and thought, "Hey, that would make a good illustration for a book I'm writing." You may not find gold every time you sit down with a book but there's gold out there.

The point is, find a creative way to open your message. It needs to tie in with the whole of your message and lay the track toward the ending. It should be something gripping. If you're using humor, you want them relaxed and open to receive. Maybe you have a story that will put them on the edge of their seats. Great, use that momentum. Can you find something that will get them asking questions in their head? If you can get them asking the questions you will answer, then you've got them. They won't be able to wait to find out what you will say. It's not just about using flashy illustrations and moving stories. You are searching for something that will give people a reason to listen, something that makes them sit up and say, "I need this."

Not only will you spend more time preparing your opening but you should spend the most time going over it too. I talk about this more in the Law of the Drill. But you need to go over your opening so you can share it without notes. The reason for this is that if you can nail the opening the rest of the message will fall in place. So you need to do everything you can to be sure you nail it.

Distractions come. Kids will cry as soon as you walk to the pulpit. There is always a transition time before you preach, ushers are walking out because someone just took the offering. Some people think that's their chance to use the bathroom, on their way they stop and talk too loudly to someone. How do you handle these distractions? If you have your opening down so you can do it without notes, you can just keep on trucking right through the distractions. If you have to pause for a distraction, you can pick it right back up. Nothing will shake you and you should be good to go through the rest of the message.

So let me say, preach to be heard. Use the Law of the Tee Off to your advantage and people will listen to what you have to say.

NUTS & BOLTS

- *Keep your eyes open*

    Be on the lookout for tee-off items. These can be true or humorous stories, something that happened to you or someone you know, videos, music, etc.

- *Start a file*

    When you come across something that would be a good starter file it away. Maybe it doesn't fit what you're doing this week but it might be great for a later message. When you use something from your file make a note of the date. It's ok to go back to it another time but be sure its had time to breathe.

- *Review*

    Once you have your tee-off be sure to spend time with it. Go over it until you know it well and can share it without any notes. This doesn't mean you have to memorize it. The goal is to be able to share the heart of your opener without reading it.

THE LAW OF THE BIG PICTURE
Good communicators don't just speak, they paint a picture

Harriet Beecher Stowe's story changed the world. It was just a story, but it touched the heart of the nation. There is a rumor that when she met President Lincoln, he shook her hand and said, "So you're the little woman who wrote the book that started this great war." It's not clear if Lincoln ever said those words but what is clear is that her book, Uncle Tom's Cabin helped bring an end to slavery in the United States.

Never underestimate the power of a story.

Stories have been part of every culture from the beginning of history until now. Before there was recorded history there was the story. Maybe you read Beowulf in school or watched a movie based on the book. That story is the oldest surviving epic poem in the English language, it was written around 1,000 A.D. Why would something that reads like one of Dr. Seuss's nightmares survive for so long? It's the story. We were wired for stories. We like a good story.

> "STORIES ARE THE CREATIVE CONVERSION OF LIFE ITSELF INTO A MORE POWERFUL, CLEARER, MORE MEANINGFUL EXPERIENCE. THEY ARE THE CURRENCY OF HUMAN CONTACT."
> -Robert McKee

THE LION THE WITCH AND THE WARDROBE

No one understood this better than C.S. Lewis. Lewis was not only an incredible children's author but as you probably know, he was an incredible theologian. Mere Christianity is one of the most thought provoking theological works I've ever read. But it's his children's stories that made him famous. What was it about them that captured the hearts of so many children, and adults? I remember a teacher reading his book, The Lion, the Witch and the Wardrobe to a class when I was young. It was amazing. I read it again many years later, it still moved me. When Aslan gave his life for Edmund, I was in tears.

Everyone who reads those books or watches those movies has one character they walk away thinking about. He's the star. The big ferocious lion, who can also be so kind that he allows two girls to ride on his back. The White Witch didn't stand a chance. Children often wrote to Lewis asking questions about Narnia and the characters he mentions. One child wrote and asked about Aslan. Who was he? Lewis didn't come right out and give simple answers. He wanted children to learn to think through his story. He gave this answer about Aslan,

> *"Has there ever been anyone in this world who (1) arrived at the same time as Father Christmas; (2) said he was the son of the Great Emperor; (3) gave himself up for someone else's fault to be jeered at and killed by wicked people; (4) came to life again; (5) is sometimes spoken of as a Lamb… don't you really know His name in this world? Think it over and let me know your answer!*[16]

Lewis knew the power of a story to illustrate a message. Jesus used stories. In fact most of the time Jesus spoke He was telling a story. He was good at it. Someone asked him a question once, "What must I do to inherit eternal life?"

Jesus answered, "Love the Lord your God with all your heart, with all your soul, with all your strength, and with all your mind; and your neighbor as yourself."

The man thought about it but wanted to "justify himself". There's a preaching point right there but I'm going to let it pass. He asked Jesus this next question, "And who is my neighbor?"[17]

Things haven't changed much in two thousand years. People still want to justify themselves. How do you define neighbor?

Jesus could have just told him that means everyone

you come in contact with, or something along those lines, but He used the question to launch into the story of the Good Samaritan. A story we all know. It's a powerful story. The man who asked the question, instead of leaving feeling justified, probably left with a new question. Did he love his neighbor as much as he loved himself? The story touches our hearts. We feel compassion for the man who is beaten. We're angry at the religious people who pass him by. And when the Samaritan stops we want to cheer. It would have struck a different chord at the time as Jews didn't associate with Samaritans. The point of the story is hard to miss. It gives more than a simple answer. It makes us feel. But it does something more, it paints a picture.

THE BOB ROSS OF PREACHING

It's that picture that helps us realize the point of the story, or in our case the point of the message. We've been preaching, we're sharing a spiritual truth that has a huge impact on the lives of everyone in the room, but are they getting it. Do they understand how important this is? Is it real to them? That's where the Big Picture comes in. You become the Bob Ross of preaching as you paint a picture that illustrates what you've been saying.

"DON'T BE AFRAID TO GO OUT ON A LIMB, BECAUSE THAT'S WHERE THE FRUIT IS."

-Bob Ross

The Big Picture is the highlighter of our message.

We use these tools to highlight a spiritual truth. We take that truth and explain it using something from the real world that everyone can understand.

I came across an illustration I use often, usually when I'm speaking on a missions trip. The team I work with and I get invited to a lot of schools when we travel overseas. When I close out the time I tell the students a story. Let me share it in a nutshell:

Every day a bus driver would drive up a steep mountain road. He picked up students at the top and then he drove back down the other side. The road is full of twists and turns. Many times the driver must slow the bus until it is almost stopped to navigate the turn. At one of these turns there is a fence with a field on the other side. Every day a little boy is sitting on that fence waiting to see the bus. The boy waves as the bus drives past. The driver slows the bus to make the turn and honks as he passes the boy. The children don't notice the boy, they are busy looking down the steep cliff on the other side. One day while bus is moving down the hill the driver steps on the brakes to slow the bus down but the brakes don't work. The bus picks up speed. The driver knows the bus will drive off the edge of the mountain and everyone will die unless he can steer through the fence to the field. But now he can already see the little boy, waving.

The driver knows the only way to save the children on his bus is to sacrifice the little boy. As he gets closer, he closes his eyes and turns the wheel into the fence, killing the boy instantly. The bus crashes through the fence and slows to a stop on the other side. The children do not understand what happened. They get off the bus one at a time, swearing at the "crazy driver" who almost killed them. They don't realize he saved their lives. The man holds head in his hands weeping as the police arrive.

"It's ok." The police tell him when they hear the story. "You're a hero. You saved all these children. It was just one boy who died."

"You don't understand," the man replied. "That boy was my son."[18]

A father gave his son so many could live. That's what God did for us. He sent his only Son to die so we wouldn't have to. Some people are like those children. They don't understand what God has done for them. But He is waiting with open arms. You get the point. It's a story. It isn't a perfect allegory, but the point is John 3:16. God gave up His Son so we could live. When I share this at the end of my time at a school, the students remember the story. It moves them and makes them feel. They are angry at those children who curse the driver. They don't want to be like them. That's not manipulation, it's helping them think through a choice. Who do I want to be? What would I do?

Your sermon needs good illustrations. It doesn't have to be a story. But a good story helps us feel your message. An illustration is anything you take from one world and bring in to another to highlight a spiritual truth. It could be something from your everyday life or like C.S. Lewis something from Narnia. It could be something that happened to you or it might be something you read about.

The story might be from the Bible. It might be your text for the message. If so, tell it like a story. You can read parts of it but try to relate as much of the text as you can like you are sitting around a campfire telling a good story. Make us feel the story so we can feel your message. Paint the picture.

There is an art to storytelling that takes time to develop. The only way to get this down is practice. Have you ever heard a joke and then tried to repeat it later only to botch the punch line? Or worse, maybe you've started the joke but for the life of you, you can't remember how it ends. How do some people just seem to know how to deliver a joke or tell a great story? The answer is practice. If you told that same joke ten times you'd have it down. In fact you would improve on it because as you tell it to yourself you'd think of better ways to say it. You'd come up with just the right delivery. You'd nail the place to "pause for effect." It's the same with a story.

To tell a great story you can't read it. It's got to come out of you. When your preaching takes you to a story in the Word of God share that story like you would an actual story. You can only do that when you know the story well and have practiced it. But it's so much better to hear a great story than have someone read it. We are wired for stories, use them well. They will help you paint the picture of your sermon.

NUTS & BOLTS

- *Read*

    Just like with the tee-off you are on the lookout for great big picture material. Becoming an avid reader is one of the best ways to find new illustrations. I love the Readers Digest, every issue has real-life stories that make great sermon material. You can find illustrations everywhere if you look hard enough but being a reader is one of the best ways.

- *Start a file (again)*

    You already have a tee-off file, right? Start a big picture file. Your files can overlap if you want but I like to keep them separate. If you read something copy it down, cite it, and file it away. Organize your file by categories. This can be tough because a lot of your material will work for multiple topics but put it where it fits best and hopefully you will have it when you need it.

THE LAW OF THE MIRROR
Hold up a mirror for people to see that the message is for them.

A good message must be more than just a transfer of information. It has to become real to each person. There has to be something in a sermon that makes people realize they need what you have to offer. They need to see the message is for them. At some point your message needs a mirror moment. It's the moment when you show them the message is about them. They need to see themselves in the message. If they don't understand the message is for them, they will not connect with it.

Imagine a couple is in counseling because they are having problems in their marriage. Neither person seems to understand where they might be part of the conflict. All they can see is what the other person has done or is doing. They aren't able to make the connection and see they are part of the problem until the counselor shines a light on the situation. Sometimes preaching is like that.

You are preaching about something that most if not everyone needs and those who need it the most think you're preaching to someone else.

"Hey that was a great message there, Pastor. I'm going to get me a copy of that and take it to my brother. He really needs to hear that. He's such a jerk."

When a person cannot connect a message to their own life, they can't figure out what to do with it. They don't mind listening. It seems like good information. But they don't know what to do with it. That's why every message needs mirror moments. There must be a point where those who listen sit up and realize, "Hey, he's talking about me!"

YOU'RE THE MAN

King David had one of those moments. Remember when David had slept with Bathsheba. Later he found out she was pregnant and had her husband killed. It's a sad story but a great example of a mirror moment happens when the Prophet Nathan comes to visit David. He paints a picture with a story which is just an illustration for David's sin.

The prophet tells about a rich man and a poor man. The rich man had everything he needed. He had more than enough of everything. But the poor man had nothing but a small lamb. The poor man cared for that lamb like it was his child. He looked after it and fed it by hand. It was everything to him.

I can see King David connecting with this story. He's probably thinking back to the days of his youth when he worked as a shepherd. Maybe he had lambs he would carry around like pets. He can relate to this poor man.

The prophet continues his story. One day a traveler came to stay with the rich man. It was customary to prepare a meal for travelers who lodged with someone. The wealthy man could have taken his choice of hundreds of his own animals to slaughter and serve to the man. Instead he went to the poor man and stole his sheep. He slaughtered, cooked and served the poor man's pet lamb to his guest.

David was full of rage. "As the LORD lives, the man who did this deserves to die!"

He was getting the Big Picture. An illustration is a powerful thing. But it can't stop there. If the prophet had turned and walked away the message wouldn't have hit home.

Nathan looks at David and says, "You are the man!"[19]

Then he delivers a word from the Lord to David. It must have been a heart-stopping moment. I can imagine him grabbing his chest and falling onto his throne just like Fred Sanford. This was David's mirror moment. The moment when he realized the message was for him. It clicked right away in his brain. He stole a woman away from her husband. If the man who stole a lamb deserved to die, what did he deserve? Aren't you glad God doesn't treat us like we deserve?

The mirror moments don't and shouldn't always be negative. They can be used to point out sin if that's what you're preaching about. But more than that they highlight everything you're talking about. The mirror moment points out what God wants to do in the life of each individual.

The mirror moment also let's people know how to use what you're talking about.

If I'm driving down the road and see flashing lights behind me my heart races. I slow down and get out of the way. I might think about some people who passed me on the road. Those guys are about to get it. But if those lights pull up right behind me and stop when I stop, I know I'm about to get it. I'm watching in my mirror hoping the car will just drive away but if it doesn't I know those lights are for me.

"IF YOU LOOK INTO THE MIRROR AND DON'T LIKE WHAT YOU SEE, DON'T BLAME THE MIRROR."

So with your mirror moments your job is to convey how the message is for your audience. That can be tough because you have a lot of different people in the room. They all have different struggles and situations they are facing. One might wonder how do they deal with their problem child. Another might struggle in their marriage. Another is wondering how to pay the bills. Some are dealing with sin issues and some are away from the Lord. How do you make your message fit every person?

The answer is you can't. But you should try to apply your message to as many situations as possible. For instance if you're preaching about the peace of God then maybe you say something like, "No matter what situation you might be facing, financial, health issues, marital problems or anything else; God can give you peace in the middle of your storm…"

Sometimes just mentioning a specific situation is enough to let people realize what you're talking about fits what they are going through. They hear a key word like, *finances, family situations, health battles*, etc. and they perk up, because they are dealing with that. You can't assume they will make the connection for the situation they are facing. They might think about it but then they wonder if what you're saying fits into their life. Give them reassurance you're talking to them.

You should have several of these moments throughout your message. There needs to be a connection to what's being said early on. You don't want to leave people hanging until the end and then show them how it all fits. Show them early and they'll pay attention to what you're saying. Keep them connected throughout by showing them how each part of your message fits into their lives.

Let me use the salesman analogy again. Imagine a salesman is selling a car to a family. The mom has been frustrated with her car. She hates that there are not enough cup holders. There are always cups all over the floor. Dad wants a car with a better sound system. The system in his old car only plays CD's, but he wants to use Bluetooth and connect his phone. The kids don't care what they get, they're not going to like it.

If the salesman shows the family the engine and focuses on the horsepower for about twenty minutes and then he spends another ten minutes telling them about the suspension what will happen? They will walk away. It's not what they need. It's part of the car but doesn't fit where they are. The salesman needs to show a lot of different things about the car. If he's able to find out what they're looking for he can point those things out. But if he doesn't know he needs to show a lot of things about the car.

The mirror moment is a little like that. Unless you know what everyone in the room is going through (and you never will) then you need to show many facets to your message. Your message will always fit many situations you just have to find some that fit best and point out how they fit.

BE A DOER

The next task is to show how to use what you just told them.

It's great to hear Jesus can save me. What do I need to do?

I can be set free from my addiction. How?

I don't have to be depressed any more? But I still feel depressed. What do I do?

This is huge. We have to show people how to put the Word of God to work in their lives. It's not enough just to hear God wants to help them. They need to know how to act on what they've heard. After all, we're told to not just be hearers of the Word but to be doers. To do the Word, we have to know what we are supposed to do.

"KNOWLEDGE IS LIKE PAINT. IT DOES NOTHING UNLESS IT IS APPLIED."

I have an uncle who teaches courses for plumbers. He was a plumber for many years and has done every plumbing job imaginable. He knows his stuff. But his job is to make sure that not only do his students know their stuff but that they can do the job. It's one thing to know what a pipe wrench is, it's another thing altogether to know how to use one. If he never teaches how apply the knowledge, well I wouldn't want any of them working on my toilets.

We can't just teach about the Word of God, we must teach and preach how to put that Word to work in our lives. We must give clear instructions on how to live and what to do with the message we have been preaching.

Our job is to show people what the Word says about them and then show them what the Word says to do about it. The Word will tell us how to live. Your job is to show them what the Word says. Give them mirror moments. The Word of God is the ultimate mirror. If you present it, people will be forced to look at their own lives and that is where transformation happens. When we can see ourselves in light of God's Word we will want to be changed, transformed to be more like Him.

NUTS & BOLTS

- *Remember the needs*

  As you began writing your message you identified needs people will have. Now you are holding up a mirror so they can see the need they have in their lives.

  If you are preaching about peace in the storm you now need to reveal their need for peace. Ask if they wake up in the morning and immediately wrestle with thoughts of worry, fear and doubt. Do they have trouble sleeping because they are consumed with the same thoughts? Are they struggling with depression? Hold up the mirror so they realize their own need.

- *What to do about it*

  They see they have a need and you have the solution. Show them what to do about it. "You have been struggling with depression, fear and worry… the Word of God says to cast your cares on Him because He cares for you…"

  Don't leave them hanging. You showed them the mirror now give them the answer to the problem.

THE LAW OF THE CATALYST
Preaching must lead to change

Good sermons have something in common with good books or good movies. There is a moment when life changes for the character. They must decide to continue with life as they know it or make a drastic change. It's the moment when the character becomes the hero. It's called the catalyst moment.

In the movie Spiderman, the main character get's his wall-climbing, web-shooting powers. But the catalyst moment is when he finds out his uncle was murdered and he could have stopped it. It's that moment Spiderman decides to become Spiderman.

You name the movie, or the book, there will always be a catalyst moment. Should I or shouldn't I? If I do my world will get flipped upside-down. It's the moment of decision.

> "WHATEVER SUBJECT I PREACH, I DO NOT STOP UNITL I REACH THE SAVIOR, THE LORD JESUS, FOR IN HIM ARE ALL THINGS."
>
> -Charles Spurgeon

In the Bible a catalyst moment comes to mind in Joshua 24. Joshua had led Israel into the promised land. Battles had been fought and people had settled in the land. Now Joshua's time is almost over. He calls the people together and reminds them of all that God had done for them. Then he comes to the catalyst moment:

> And if it seem evil unto you to serve the LORD, choose you this day whom ye will serve; whether the gods which your fathers served that were on the other side of the flood, or the gods of the Amorites, in whose land ye dwell: but as for me and my house, we will serve the LORD.[20]

The catalyst moment is the *choose this day* moment of your message. Everything you've said until now has led to this one moment in time. It's the call to action. It's the decision that will change lives forever. Every good sermon needs one.

I mentioned in an earlier chapter about always

offering a call to salvation. You might look at a message and think, "It's not a salvation message." Not true. Every word of Scripture points to the cross. Always give people a chance to decide. But also recognize not everyone in the room needs to get saved every week, so don't preach like they do. But they need other things. So make your altar call fit your message.

You can have many catalyst moments in your life. Remember Peter? Jesus called him to be a disciple. He left everything to follow Jesus. It was his catalyst moment. Then later in Acts 2 he is filled with the Holy Spirit, stands up and preaches boldly. This is the same guy who denied Jesus a few weeks before, now he is filled with boldness. What happened to him? He had a catalyst moment when the Holy Spirit filled him.

Now look what the people say after he preaches, "When they heard this, they came under deep conviction and said to Peter and the rest of the apostles: "Brothers, what must we do?"[21]

They heard the message Peter had preached about Jesus. He tells them they had killed the Messiah but God had raised him up. They were so convicted they didn't want to hear the rest of the message. If they were in chairs, they probably jumped up as they shouted, "What do we need to do!" They were crying out for a catalyst moment. They didn't want to hear and walk away, they knew they needed to be changed.

The catalyst moment is about change.

Now not every sermon calls for life-altering

transformation but every sermon should offer a call to action. If not go back to the Law of the Spear and find your point! Your point should include a call to action, a decision, a catalyst moment. That doesn't mean every week everyone has to be rushing the altar, but that's great if they do. Sometimes a catalyst moment might be a simple prayer together.

"THE TEST OF A PREACHER IS THAT HIS CONGREGATION GOES AWAY SAYING, NOT 'WHAT A LOVELY SERMON,' BUT, 'I WILL DO SOMETHING.'"
-Francis De Sales

The heart of the catalyst moment is for people to decide to act on what you've been preaching about. Knowledge without action doesn't equal change. Remember the story of King David. His life is changed when the prophet Samuel shows up at his house and anoints him as king.

It's an interesting moment. This boy is now the king. The only problem is Israel already has a king. David has to wait until it's his time. But the catalyst moment has come. The change is already in him. It doesn't seem obvious to his father, he just kicks him out back to keep watching the sheep. But the boy is changed.

You see it later, when David is sent to check on his brothers, who are at war. He sees a giant come out and taunt Israel's soldiers. The kingly anointing rises inside him and he knows he has to do something. He walks up to

King Saul, and he tells him he will go face the giant.

Saul thinks the boy is crazy, "You can't go fight this Philistine. You're just a youth, and he's been a warrior since he was young."

But David answers, *"Your servant has been tending his father's sheep."*

Now that's not a great way to start when you're giving your qualifications to go fight a giant. That's not a great resume. But look what he says next.

"Whenever a lion or a bear came and carried off a lamb from the flock, I went after it, struck it down, and rescued the lamb from its mouth. If it reared up against me, I would grab it by its fur, strike it down, and kill it. Your servant has killed lions and bears; this uncircumcised Philistine will be like one of them, for he has defied the armies of the living God."[22]

Now Saul knows this boy is crazy. Notice, he doesn't say, "one time a lion came." He says *"Whenever a lion came."* In other words, this happened a lot. And if the lion or bear turned on him, he would grab it by the fur and strike it down. Imagine the scene. Here comes a lion, how many of us would run after it? David did. David had a moment where everything changed. He wasn't just a forgotten boy in the fields anymore. God had anointed him. He was walking in his anointing before he was ever in a position.

He would grab lions and bears by their beards and strike them. It doesn't say what he would strike them with but it sounds like it was with his fist. He just went to town on these wild animals punching them until they were dead. It's hard to imagine that kind of courage. But it was practice for what was coming.

The point is, that David had a catalyst moment. Without that moment his life would have gone on like normal. Nothing extraordinary would have happened. But because of that one moment the course of his life changed.

People need catalyst moments, moments to decide to chase the call God has for their lives, or to continue with life as normal. How you implement this law is up to you but as always, creativity is important. If you are a pastor, you don't want to always do things the same way, week in and week out. You need to switch it up. Some services might call for a longer time in prayer together at the front of the room. But you might not want to do that every week, depending on your congregation.

If you are an evangelist or someone who preaches in a lot of different places, you have more freedom. You can do the same thing every time because you're always speaking to different people.

No matter how you put your catalyst moment together the important thing is that you have one and that it points toward something specific. You must make sure it fits in well with your message. Don't preach about how to be a witness and then ask people to work on loving their spouse. It needs to tie in with the message.

Present an opportunity to do something with what you just preached. For example,

You heard me preaching about forgiveness today. As I've been speaking there is someone coming to your mind that you have struggled to forgive. That person may have hurt you, but today God is calling you to walk in forgiveness. Forgive like He has forgiven you.

Or maybe it would be as simple as this,

We spoke about laying everything on the altar today. Today as we sing this song make it a declaration that you are laying that thing down.

You know what fits your message and your congregation. I'm not telling you to do something big and showy, that's not what this is about. But it is about giving people a chance to decide. Maybe it's the decision to love our families like Jesus loves us. Send them home with a love challenge.

Do one thing each day this week for your family to show them the love of Jesus. Fix breakfast, write a love letter, play a game...

The long and short of it is our preaching needs to be more than just hearing about the Word of God it needs to help us do what the Word of God says and live the way the Word tells us to live.

I was watching the news one morning, and I heard an interview with a man who had a catalyst moment in his life. The day he was born his father walked out on him. His mother was lying in the hospital in tears. Along with feeling hurt she was also now facing the realization she would be raising a child by herself. What hit her the hardest at that moment was that no one could sign the birth certificate as the father. She called a friend in the military who happened to be in town. The man agreed to come and sign the birth certificate.

She was so appreciative she named her son after the man. It wasn't until years later when her son was in high school that he learned how he got his name. She told him the story and said she wanted to introduce them. The young man felt a deep appreciation. It was a catalyst moment in his life. He realized his name was not his own. His name was given to honor this man. When he stepped up to meet the man, he shook his hand and told him, "I will make your name great."[23]

That young man was Ray Lewis Jr. and he grew up to become an incredible athlete and played in the NFL for many years.

His story has stuck with me. See, we don't have our own names anymore. We've been given a new name. Now we are part of the family of God. Our mission in life is to make His name great. That one catalyst moment changed Ray Lewis Jr. It gave him purpose. The goal of our preaching is to give people a chance for those same kind of moments.

NUTS & BOLTS

- *Start with the ending*

    A good story has to be going somewhere. Before you even start writing your sermon, know where it's going. You are leading people to a catalyst moment. Keep that ending in sight as you preach. Let them know it's coming.

- *Get to the action*

    Give them a chance to act on what they just heard. Lead a salvation call. Even if the sermon wasn't specifically about salvation, start there. Next provide practical applications for what you preached on. If the message was about loving your spouse don't just tell them to love their spouse, ask them to commit to a demonstration of love every day during the week. Give them ideas like: breakfast in bed, helping out around the house (if they don't normally), buying flowers, etc.

THE LAW OF HOPE
Don't forget the good in the good news

Flagstaff, Main was just a small dot on a map that was about to disappear. Engineers had been planning a new lake that would provide water for the area and it so happened Flagstaff was in the wrong place. The people who lived there had plenty of time to move but most stayed for as long as possible.

Something interesting happened in Flagstaff. Yards became overgrown even though people still lived there. After all, who wants to take care of a yard that will be underwater? Houses fell into a state of disrepair because who wants to fix a house that's about to be full of fish. Day after day, week after week the town grew worse. Flagstaff looked like a ghost town, except people still lived there.

Someone who had spent time in the area made this observation about Flagstaff. He said, "Where there is no faith in the future, there is no power in the present."[24] That is true for our lives. When someone gives up hope for the future, it is obvious in their present life. What is true for our lives is also true for our preaching. If we don't offer hope we haven't preached the Gospel. There are people walking into churches every week feeling discouraged and depressed. They might be there looking for something to give them hope. If they leave the same way they came in, then we haven't done our jobs.

The Law of Hope says, don't forget the good, in the good news. Preach the Gospel and people will be filled with hope.

"SO NOW WE MUST CLING TIGHTLY TO THE HOPE THAT LIVES WITHIN US, KNOWING THAT GOD ALWAYS KEEPS HIS PROMISES."

-Hebrews 10:23 (TPT)

GOOD NEWS

The Gospel is good news. Jesus came to preach good news. But how often do we leave the good out of our messages? The Gospel gives hope for a future. People don't have to leave wallowing in their past, they can leave rejoicing because they have a hope and a future. Look at what Jesus said about His preaching,

He came to Nazareth, where He had been brought

> up. As usual, He entered the synagogue on the Sabbath day and stood up to read. The scroll of the prophet Isaiah was given to Him, and unrolling the scroll, He found the place where it was written:
>
> The Spirit of the Lord is on Me,
> because He has anointed Me
> to preach good news to the poor.
> He has sent Me
> to proclaim freedom to the captives
> and recovery of sight to the blind,
> to set free the oppressed, to proclaim the year of the Lord's favor.
>
> He then rolled up the scroll, gave it back to the attendant, and sat down. And the eyes of everyone in the synagogue were fixed on Him. He began by saying to them, "Today as you listen, this Scripture has been fulfilled."[25]

Jesus reads Isaiah and says He is anointed to preach *good news*. That's the Gospel. The word Gospel literally means good news. Some preachers don't have that anointing. They seem to have an anointing to preach bad news.

Does that mean we can't preach about sin and hell? Of course not, Jesus spoke about hell. But the message should be: *you don't have to go to hell. There's hope for you!* There must be hope. Our preaching MUST bring hope. If we don't have hope we don't have the Gospel, we only have judgment. We're stuck in the Old Testament and have forgotten about the blood of Jesus that can save and set free.

Look at that verse again. He says He was anointed to bring freedom to captives, recovery of sight to the blind and freedom for the oppressed. It's all good news. His message was: *Are you bound in sin, depression, fear, worry, anxiety, etc.? I've come to set you free.*

I love the last part of the verse. He says He was anointed to proclaim the year of the Lord's favor. This is a reference to the year of jubilee. Jubilee was the fiftieth year in the Jewish calendar where slaves would be freed. Debts were canceled. Property was returned to the original owner. It was a festive, joy filled time. People were in debt were looking forward to the year of jubilee. They had hope that a time was coming when it would all be erased. So Jesus shows up and says, "It's here!"

Think about what He's saying. His anointing was to declare, "JUBILEE!" That's powerful. He's saying, "Hey, you were a slave to the devil. I'm here to set you free today!"

SEARCHING FOR HOPE

It's interesting He stopped reading there because the next words in Isaiah 61 says, "and the day of our God's vengeance…"

Jesus stops reading mid sentence. Why? Why not stand there and shout about the day of God's vengeance? Because it wasn't time for that yet. His first coming was about the favor of God coming to us. The second coming is about vengeance. His anointing was to preach good news, not vengeance.

I recently read a story about a US soldier in WWII. His plane crashed in the ocean. After breaking a record for the longest time spent in a life raft he and the other guy with him were picked up by the Japanese and put in a POW camp. During his time there the guards seemed to have one job: to break the spirits of the men in the camp. One guard made this prisoner his pet project. Day after day he tried to break him.

It turned out the soldier was a world famous athlete, and the Japanese wanted to use him for propaganda. They had plans of him making radio and television appearances where he would criticize the US.

So the punishment continued. Day in and day out, he was beaten, tortured, and malnourished. He went through unspeakable things. But he determined within himself that he would not break. The guard tried to take away all hope for a future, but still the man held on.

We live in a world that for many people seems hopeless. Someone you might preach to this week is facing a failing marriage. It seems hopeless. Another might have lost a job and wonders how they will make it. Hopeless. Maybe someone came through your door for the first time, struggling with addiction, searching for hope, but it seems so hopeless.

We live in a fallen world that lives every day without hope. We have the cure for the disease that infects every man, woman and child ever born. People aren't walking into our buildings to find a social network or a great cup of coffee (although I like good coffee). People are coming because they are looking for hope.

"OFT HOPE IS BORN WHEN ALL IS FORLORN."
                                    -J.R.R. Tolkien

There are no hopeless situations in Christ. There are no hopeless people. When Jesus enters the equation, everything changes. Preach hope. Preach the Gospel.

NUTS & BOLTS

- *Look for hope*

    Read over your sermon. Is hope in there? I don't mean the word, hope, but the message of hope. The cross is hope. Jesus is hope. The love of God is hope. If hope's not in your message you've left out the Gospel.

- *Spread the hope*

    People who live with hope will be people who share hope. Hope is contagious. The Gospel is a contagious Gospel. Encourage your people to not just receive but to give hope.

THE LAW OF THE DRILL
Communication takes practice

Before a pilot will take a plane up, he runs through a detailed pre-flight checklist. He goes over his flight plan and checks the weather, not just where he is but where he is going and everywhere in between. He goes over the aircraft with a fine tooth comb. If something is not working, he wants to catch it on the ground before he takes it up in the air. If something malfunctions while the plane is in the air it could end in disaster. He checks his fuel, goes over the engine, cleans the windshield, checks the lights, tests the radio, and goes over a whole list of other instruments. The pilot wants to know everything works.

If pastors approached their sermons like a pilot does his airplane, the quality of our messages would skyrocket. Yes it takes time, but this is a step we CANNOT skip. At this point, you've taken the time to prepare your message. You've been chewing on the topic all week.

You've discovered big picture illustrations and brought it home with powerful applications. Time and thought have gone into the tee-off and a catalyst moment is prepared that will give an opportunity for change. That's it, right? Not yet. You don't know if it all works the way it should. Just like a pilot you need to go over everything.

THE FIRE DRILL

Remember, being in school and doing fire drills. It felt like we were doing fire drills all the time. When I moved to Springfield, Missouri for college I found out about tornado drills. We didn't have many tornados where I grew up but in Missouri they were a regular thing. The college would run tornado drills on campus. They would set off a siren to signal the drill and we all had to go squeeze in to a little basement near the cafeteria until the drill was over. It was a little annoying. I wondered why we had to bother with the drill. Until one day when a tornado alarm went off in the middle of the night. It was a scary moment. I knew it wasn't a drill. We all ran down to the basement and waited. The tornado didn't touch our campus, but I was glad we drilled.

If it hadn't been for the drill, no one would have known what to do. That's why they have all those drills. When you're prepared your training kicks in. You don't need to think about what to do. It's like muscle memory. When you do something enough, you don't even have to think about it, you do it out of habit. Now think about when you preach. Maybe you have a killer sermon, but your delivery is lacking. You're getting lost and fumbling through the message. Maybe you've been preaching for years but you still get nervous when you walk up to the pulpit, I do and I think it's perfectly normal, in those first moments of nervousness you can easily get distracted. When you're distracted or nervous, you can lose your train of thought. It can feel like your sermon has been zapped out of your head and you're staring at notes that make little sense.

"HARD WORK BEATS TALENT, WHEN TALENT DOESN'T WORK HARD."

-Tim Notke

This is where the Law of the Drill comes in. If you drill your sermon properly, when you step up to speak, it won't matter if a whole nursery full of babies starts crying, the ceiling springs a leak on someone's head (that happened in our church) and a chicken runs across the stage (I preached with one in Africa) all at the same time. When you've put the Law of the Drill into practice, you can keep preaching like nothing is happening.

I was asked to speak at a meeting once. It was an impromptu sort of thing. But I got up and said a few words. While I was speaking there was a group behind me setting up for worship. There was a lot of noise, heavy chairs were being dragged across a tile floor. There were loud conversations about which song they would play. It was a total distraction. I did my best, but I was having a hard time. I didn't know ahead of time what I would say and I'm not sure I said anything worthwhile.

The fact is distractions will happen. There will always be something to get you off track from your sermon. But the other reason for this law is that most of us write one way and speak another. If you write out your sermon word for word like some people do, when you try to preach you wind up just reading and losing some of the excitement. There needs to be a spontaneity to your message that doesn't come from reading. Not to mention that when you read a message, it will come off sounding different than you would speak, you want it to sound more conversational not like a book or a lecture.

When you go over your message a couple times, you will become more familiar with it and you will be able to say parts of it without looking at your notes at all. I'm not saying you have to memorize your message. But when you know your message well, it gives you freedom to even walk away from the pulpit for a moment and not get lost. You know where you're going because you've done the drill.

The hardest part of the message, and the most important to get right, is the intro. I mentioned this in a the Law of the Tee-Off, but I want to focus on the drill aspect. When I drill my messages, before I go through the entire sermon, I work on the tee-off. I want to get it right before I move on. I might go over it a dozen times just to be sure I like the way it sounds. I want to make sure it's tying in with the rest of the message the way I thought it did when I wrote it. I'm trying to get it to sound natural and conversational. Rarely will I read a story in my intro or in my sermon at all. If I have a great illustration that requires I read it, I might save it for later in the message.

A CONVERSATIONAL SERMON

With my intro or any illustration I want to relate it without looking at my notes. Just like if I was talking to you. It would be awkward if in the middle of telling you a story or sharing something personal with you, I had to look down to remind myself what to say next. I want it to feel natural. So I drill it. I want my sermon to sound conversational.

I know that if I can nail the intro the rest of the sermon will fall into place much easier. The intro is the time when I am most nervous. I'm walking up to the pulpit and there is the uncomfortable feeling, "How am I going to transition this thing." That feeling magnifies as you walk up and set your Bible and notes on the pulpit. You look up and everyone is staring at you and suddenly your sermon is gone. It can be an intimidating moment. I like to have something in mind for a transition depending on what was going on before I walked up. Usually there is an offering or a special music or maybe someone said something during worship or offering that was worth repeating. Or maybe there's an event coming up or something else worth noting. "How many of you parents are excited that summer is almost over and school is starting back up next week? Can I get an amen?" Just a little transitional comment helps everyone relax and then it's off to the sermon.

"GIVE ME SIX HOURS TO CHOP DOWN A TREE AND I WILL SPEND THE FIRST FOUR SHARPENING THE AXE."
                                                            -Abraham Lincoln

---

If you've drilled your intro well, you have no trouble with how to begin. You just launch into it and it should come out as you practiced. It flows out of you. That opening sentence is important. How do I launch this thing? I usually start with something like, "Take your Bibles and open to (insert your reference), while you're turning there let me tell you about something that happened this week." From there I launch into my intro. Start however you want but figuring out that transition sentence is huge. It will help you keep things sounding natural and avoid that awkward feeling.

After I have drilled my intro several times and got it to sound like I want, then I go into the rest of the message. If my message has been stewing in my head all week, I rarely need more than one run through to get it down. Sometimes I might go through the message twice because I wind up making changes as I go the first time. If I need to go through it a third time I will but that will be it. If I do it more, I will end up tweaking it too much and confuse myself.

As I walk through my message, I want focus on any illustrations and get them down so I don't have to read them unless I happen to be using something longer or something that begs to be read. I'm not trying to get it word for word, I want to get the message so I can share it in my own words. I want to read over all my scriptures so I don't stumble on them and mark them in my Bible so I can find them easily unless I've written the verse in my notes.

I hit the rest of my message the first time by forcing myself to read it. Even thought I've been chewing all week and can probably preach a message from my head I want to read what I wrote so I don't miss something. Then on my second run through I try to walk away from my notes and see how it goes. There might be an area I have to back up and go over again but that's about it.

This law may sound obvious but there will be some that think they can skip this step. Maybe someone's been preaching a while and they think they can wing it. Your sermon won't work unless you put in the work. It takes time to drill your sermon but those who skip the drill pay the price and so do the people they are speaking to. Get into a habit of drilling your sermons well.

NUTS & BOLTS

- *Pre-flight check list*

   Just like a pilot goes over his plane, go over your sermon with the same level of scrutiny. Read it over out loud and be sure it makes sense and sounds like something you would say. Be sure the sermon flows and doesn't feel like it's jumping around.

- *Rehearse*

   Now that you have read over your sermon once or twice try to preach it. Find a quiet place where you can preach without being disturbed. Make sure people know what you're doing because you might make some noise. As you go over your sermon notice places where you might need to pause. Read over your verses just like you will when you preach. Do this a couple of times.

- *Pay attention to the tee-off and big pictures*

   Spend extra time with your opener. You want to be able to nail the first few minutes of the message and get it down the way you want it. Be sure to focus on any big picture items, especially stories. Make sure you can share them or mostly share them without reading. Again the goal is being able to sound conversational. It's hard to do that if you're reading.

- *Review the catalyst*

    Make sure you spend some extra time with your catalyst as well. This is a major moment in your message so be sure you've gone over it well enough that you can share it without notes.

THE LAW OF DELIVERY
Good communication comes through good delivery

Did you ever have that teacher in high school, the one that was monotone and had a gift for making a boring subject even more boring. It seemed like my history teachers were always those guys. I remember one teacher would actually stand and read straight from the textbook in an impossible monotone voice for the entire class. It was tough. I dreaded going to that class and I can't say I learned a lot that year. It was one of those, there in body but not in mind, situations

Did that make me a bad student? I wasn't a great student anyway, but that didn't make me a bad student. It made me normal. Most people would struggle to listen to that. If you're normal, you will not want to be there. The only reason anyone would show up for that is because they have to if they want to finish school.

Have you ever sat in a sermon like that, I see you

nodding your head. We all have at some point. If you had to go listen to someone preach like that every week what would you do? You'd find a new church! It's hard to get anything from a sermon you can't even listen to. If you're sound asleep, you can't learn anything! I know because I was in that history class and I still don't know much about history. Does that make you unspiritual? Of course not! It makes you normal.

"PREACHING IS NOT A PROFESSION, IT'S A PASSION."
-Leonard Ravenhill

Now maybe you had another kind of teacher in school. Just like there are some exceptionally bad teachers out there, there are also teachers on the opposite end of the spectrum. These are the rare, extraordinary, gifted teachers. They have a way of making a subject come alive. They could be teaching about the history of mousetraps and you hang on every word. You can't wait to learn more about how the poor little mice have met their doom throughout history. These teachers make you look forward to coming to their class. You even read your textbook. These teachers inspire you to learn

Imagine listening to a preacher like that! Maybe you've heard that kind of preaching at some point. That kind of preaching inspires you. It makes you want to come back and learn more. You're inspired to go deeper in your relationship with the Lord. You're telling your friends about it. That might seem like a lot to put on the way someone delivers a sermon, but it's true.

The way we preach is as important as what we preach. Don't get me wrong, I'm not saying what we preach isn't important. But take two people preaching the same message. If one reads the sermon slowly with a monotone voice and the other preaches it with passion and excitement what will the outcome be? People will tune out the first but they'll listen to the second. It's just human nature.

It seems like there are many in the pulpit that want to ignore this. They think because they are communicating a spiritual truth they can be boring and people will have to listen to them. If you want people to listen to your message, you have to learn how to deliver it in a way that will help them listen. This is the law on which many other laws hinge. If some of these other laws will help you take your communication from a one to a four or five, the Law of Deliver will take you to a ten.

For example you might apply the Law of the Tee Off. You are using a terrific opening to your message that will help you get people's attention. But instead of communicating your opening with enthusiasm, you simply read it. The tee-off came out flat. You might have the attention of a few people but with the Law of Delivery you could have had most, if not all, listening intently.

IT'S A SMALL WORLD

We took our kids to Disney World several years ago. They were young at the time and so we took them on the ride, It's a Small World. Now in case you've never been on this ride, (you are blessed by the way, don't go, seriously don't.), Imagine thousands of creepy looking mechanical dolls singing the same song over and over and you've got the idea. After waiting in line for two or three hours in the hot Florida sun you climb into a little boat with a dozen people you've never met, and you set off on a journey through what must have been Walt Disney's nightmare.

On our magical journey the boat got stuck, and we sat in a room for twenty minutes watching the same little smiling dolls move around and sing, "It's a small world after all." I kept waiting to see that Chucky doll pop out. But it's the song that gets in your head. They sing that over and over and over. The song gets played about 1,200 times a day.[26] I think I heard it at least 1,199 but it felt like more.

A few years later we took our kids back to Disney World, because we are insane. The kids were older and a couple of them wanted to try the bigger rides. I was thrilled. We took them to Space Mountain. I thought it might be too much for them. This isn't a kiddie ride, it's an actual roller coaster but most of it is in the dark. It makes you feel like your traveling at an incredible speed and it's full of twists and turns. The ride is supposed to make you feel like you're traveling to space. Everything about it is fun and exciting. When we got off the *It's a Small World* ride I never wanted to see it again. But Space Mountain, I could ride that all day and my kids loved it.

What's the difference? They're both rides at one of the world's most popular theme parks. But one of them is terrible. It's the same old thing over and over. There is no excitement. They sing the same old song until you hate everything about it. But the other ride offers thrills and fun. It makes you want to come back and ride it again and again.

Your sermons should be more like Space Mountain and less like It's a Small World. Don't make people feel like they just got stuck on your sermon and they couldn't get out. Now, I shared my nightmare story with you. I know you don't want people to leave and share nightmare stories about you.

"I had to listen to that guy for almost an hour. It was horrible. I kept looking at the exit thinking I could make a run for it."

PASSION AND ATTITUDE

How do we put this into practice? It's great to know that you don't want to bore people but how do we make sure we're not doing that? Think back to the illustration about the teachers. You probably had one of each at some point in your life. What made the great teacher, great? She might have been an interesting speaker, but it feels like it's more than that, right? Maybe she always had some kind of fun element in the class but it's got to be more. I think two key factors are PASSION and ATTITUDE.

A great preacher is not that different from a great teacher. They are both in the business of communication. A great teacher has a love for her subject. It's this love that comes through as she teaches. She's not reading out of a book, she's sharing out of her heart.

That is the first key of great delivery. Your sermon has to be more than just a topic. I understand we communicate the Word of God and as a preacher you have a love for the Word of God. But what I'm getting at here is your specific topic or message has to be something you have a heart for. Your message needs to flow out of your heart. Your passion will be contagious. But you can't communicate with passion if you don't have a passion for the message.

This goes back to the Law of the Cud. It's easier to get a passion for a message if you find it early and have time to chew on it. But it has to go deeper than just chewing it. You need to get it inside your heart. Let the Word that you are communicating change you. That will come through as you're preaching.

The second key is attitude. What I mean is this. Let your own personality come through as you preach. It's easy to tell when someone isn't being true to who they are. I see preachers who are so buttoned up they can hardly move. You can't be yourself like that, unless you're a robot. It's not about how you dress, it's about being comfortable with who you are. People will pick up on that and it relaxes them.

"ATTITUDE IS A LITTLE THING THAT MAKES A BIG DIFFERENCE."
-Winston Churchill

They realize you're real and being yourself. This all plays in to how you deliver your message. If you can deliver a message genuinely people will listen.

THE DELIVERY ROOM

I've been in some delivery rooms. In a delivery room there are moments of pain, excitement, joy and peace, if everything is normal. As you deliver your message, there will be emotions that come up. If you're preaching a "painful" part of the message, for example talking about failures in life, then you will share that different than you would if you were communicating joy.

The way you communicate should connect with an emotion. I'm not in to emotional preaching. I don't like hype and really don't like screaming. This isn't an exhortation for emotional preaching. But your message will hit different emotions. Different people will feel different things. Be aware of when you are in a certain emotional part of the message and deliver it appropriately.

Apply the Law of Delivery to your messages. Get a passion for your message and let that shine through as you preach. Find the way that fits you and your style and deliver your message in a way that makes people want to listen.

NUTS & BOLTS

- *Practice your delivery*

    You've been drilling your message. Now as you drill pay attention to how you speak. What does your voice sound like? Try using some excitement as you preach, but don't overdo it. Are you communicating with passion? What about your attitude, does your own personality come through as you preach?

- *Use your emotions*

    What emotions come up as you read through your message? Are there parts that are sad, joyful or solemn? Can your delivery reflect that emotion? Again this is not a call to emotionalism but rather using some emotion as you preach to help communicate the message.

THE LAW OF REVIEW
Communication improves with regular review

Evaluation is a key in communication we should all use but many simply do not. There are a few keys laws that make the difference between a good communicator and a great one, and the Law of Review is one of those.

How often do we take time to review a message? Most of the time we tell ourselves we're too busy thinking about the next one. Besides who wants to go back and listen to themselves speak. It's a horrible experience. It doesn't matter how great a speaker you are or if you are a seasoned, sought after communicator, you probably hate hearing yourself speak. The only thing worse than that is watching yourself on video. But that is exactly what great communicators do.

That doesn't mean great communicators are egomaniacs that love the sound of their own voices. It means they understand how important it is to review a message. That doesn't mean you have to do this every time you preach but it should become a regular habit.

REVIEW THE PLAY

I like watching football on a Sunday afternoon. My wife even surprised me last year for my birthday and took me to a Carolina Panthers game. It was exciting to be there in the stands cheering on my team with thousands of fans. When one team scores a touchdown, the rule in the NFL is that the play goes into review. An official will go to a screen and watch footage of the play in slow motion. He's looking for anything that might make a difference in the play. Did the player have possession? Did the ball cross the goal line? If he finds any problems, he could change the ruling on the field.

Sometimes what feels like a goal when you preach might not seem that way when you watch it back. I understand that we are our own worst critics, so be careful with this and don't let it become discouraging. But as you review your sermon try to put yourself in the congregation. Make notes as you listen. What did you do well? It's ok to give yourself some encouragement, in fact I insist. But also make notes on where you can improve.

I would caution against asking anyone to help you with this if they are a part of your congregation. It's surprising how quickly people can turn into critics. If you let someone voice their opinions about you, something snaps inside and things get critical fast. Just look at movie reviews or book reviews (hopefully not for this one!), read some things people post. People who have no movie experience want to point out everything wrong with the movie. Someone who has never written a book becomes a professional book critic. It's the same with your sermon. Don't give anyone that opportunity.

It's like those stickers you see on the back of trucks: HOW'S MY DRIVING? CALL 1-800-MY-DRIVING-IS TERRIBLE, because that's the only reason you'd ever call. No one ever calls those numbers to say, "Hey that guy driving your truck is incredible behind the wheel. He's driving the speed limit, using his turn signals and I could see him checking his mirrors before he changed lanes."

If you have a friend or mentor who is not part of your church, then by all means, ask for pointers. You can and should review your message yourself and now that you've read this book you have a great idea of what you're looking for. But asking someone else to take a look will give you a unique perspective.

"IF YOU ASK ME HOW YOU MAY SHORTEN YOUR SERMONS, I SHOULD SAY, STUDY THEM BETTER... WE ARE GENERALLY LONGEST WHEN WE HAVE LEAST TO SAY."

-Charles Spurgeon

STICK TO YOUR BUDGET

You probably have a budget for your household. I'm sure you have one for your ministry. Treat the evaluation process like you would a budget. Do you look at your budget every day? Probably not, there's no need for that. If you are about to make a big purchase, you should look at it. Otherwise the only time you check your budget is when it's time to review.

How do you review a budget? You sit down with your budget in one hand and your expenses in the other. You walk down the columns one at a time and see if there are any problems. What happens if you find a problem? Maybe you overspent in one area last month. You evaluate it. What was the reason? Is it going to be an ongoing increase? If so I have to find a place I can take that money from. Where can I cut back?

You get the idea. So I don't look at every sermon I preach. There are some that I never want to see again anyway. But the idea is to take one (or more if I'm feeling bold) of my sermons each month and listen to it. I'm listening for things I did well and things I need to improve. As I listen, I want to pay attention to my delivery. I can tell by looking at paper if I had some elements we've discussed but I can only check my delivery by reviewing my message.

Again this might feel painful but no pain no gain. Right? This is how you improve. You put yourself in the audience. Is the message coming across like you thought it did? Did you hit the points you wanted to? What emotions are you feeling? If you're watching a video, how do you look? Are you stiff or casual? Body language is important. Is your body saying the same thing as your message?

Again let me go to the sports analogy. Teams will watch hours and hours of footage. They'll watch footage of themselves and footage of the opposing team they will be facing. The point is the footage will reveal flaws they might not have noticed during the game.

In the middle of a game adrenaline is rushing. The noise from the stands pulses through your ears. There are a lot of people on the field and it's hard to follow what's happening, until they go to the footage. If someone made a great play, they want to watch it on film. Why? The goal is to see what was done well and encourage that so it happens more often. If someone messed up, the team still wants to watch. They want to make sure they don't repeat mistakes.

How many times do we repeat our mistakes in our sermons? There are things we could have corrected sooner if we would have reviewed more often. Sometimes as I'm preaching I catch myself saying something I shouldn't. It might just be a little thing that slips out but at the moment I think, *I shouldn't have said that*. By the end of the message I've forgotten what it was. That's just one reason to watch the footage. You're looking for things you didn't catch or things you did but have forgotten. Since you're making notes on the whole thing it's getting reinforced.

"That was bad! Don't do that!"

"That was really good! Do that again!"

I have some teachings we use on a recurring basis with some excellent speakers. One of them is an incredible, sought after speaker. The video we use is topnotch. But I notice he has phrases he repeats over and over. It seemed like something to say when you're not sure what to say. He would say something like, "Are you following what I'm saying?" That's not bad by itself. The problem was he might have said it 100 times in the video series.

Now I'm sure there are worse things I do but I noticed his because I have watched his videos so often. Then I saw a video he did that was filmed several years later. Guess what. He didn't use his catchphrase. Somewhere down the line I'm sure he watched his video and realized he used that phrase like a crutch and so he broke himself of the habit.

That's what happens when you watch yourself. You'll only improve. This guy didn't have much he could have improved on. That small thing was about the only flaw in his preaching. But if you want to improve, you have to listen to what your saying and how you're saying it.

It's hard to sit down and assess your preaching. But when you do, there will be things you pick up right away. You will notice things you do or say without thinking. There will be awkward pauses. You might catch yourself standing in a funny posture or repeating gestures too often. These aren't huge things but they are things you'll notice. It might be overwhelming to think of what you should look for. So I've included a review sheet at the end of the chapter to give you an idea how to approach this.

Let me give you some practical guidelines as you begin the review process. Don't fill out your review from memory on what you preached. Try to listen as if you've never heard it before. Go through each section of your message. I've given you a couple questions for some main areas but you'll want to make notes on how you did in other areas. Use the worksheet and rate yourself with the questions given. How did you do? Where do you need improvement? Don't be too hard on yourself but try to take an honest look at where you are.

As you implement the Law of Review, you will see improvement in your messages. Take the time and make this a habit in your schedule. The more you review yourself the better you will become.

NUTS & BOLTS

- *Review your message*

   Find a time once a month that you can review one or more of your messages. Try not to be too close to the message you are reviewing. For instance don't pick a message you just preached yesterday to review. The best option is to watch the video. Have someone record it if it's not already.

- *Use the checklist*

   You know a good sermon when you hear it but if part of a message wasn't working you need to know why. I've included a checklist for you on the next page to help you as you review. There are a few main areas you want to watch for. Use the checklist but don't beat yourself up about. The point is to be constantly improving.

- *Make notes in your preaching notebook*

   You need to remember where you need to improve. Write down your thoughts about your sermon in your preaching notebook. Include the things you did well along with areas you want to improve. Refer to these before you preach as a reminder.

MESSAGE REVIEW

Rate each element of the message from 1 – 10

Title:

Date:

The Law of the Spear
The point is obvious within the first few minutes. _____
The theme carries throughout the message. _____
Notes:

The Law of the Tee Off
The opening captured my attention. _____
The intro flowed with the theme of the message. _____
Notes:

The Law of the Big Picture
Illustrations brought light to the point. _____
There were an appropriate amount of illustrations. _____
Notes:

The Law of the Mirror
Applications were used several times during the message. _____
Applications could have applied to many different situations. _____
Notes:

The Law of the Catalyst
The catalyst moment was clear and specific. _____
The catalyst moment fit well with the theme. _____

Notes:

The Law of Delivery

Rate the overall delivery of the message. _____
The delivery was engaging and kept you listening. _____
Notes:

Overview

List what was done well:
List areas that needed improvement:

THE LAW OF GROWTH
Don't just survive, learn to thrive

I was in the middle of Alabama and had stopped at a roadside attraction with my family. While we were there, I noticed a cutout of a redwood tree. It was enormous. The sign said the tree had been cut down in the 1950's but someone had taken the time to count the rings of the tree and create a timeline based on the tree's lifespan. As you know, every ring represents a year in the life of a tree. How large it grows depends on a lot of factors. But every year there should be growth.

As I looked at the rings of the tree, you could see years when the tree flourished and then there were other years when the tree didn't seem to grow at all. But every year there was a mark, a little ring representing the tree's life. This tree's life spanned over 2,500 years.

There were signs on the tree marking when world events were taking place. When that tree was a sapling Confucius was coming on the scene. Hundreds of rings later Jesus was born. Keep following the rings out and you'd find Mohammed, the Alexandrian Library burned, Charlemagne crowned, The Magna Carta, Joan of Arc, then Columbus. This tree was almost 2,000 years old by the time the America's were being settled by Europeans. This tree was alive and thriving from before Jesus walked this earth all the way through the American Revolution, the discovery of electricity, World Wars I & II. And every year it was growing.

There is a tree in the same family named the General Sherman tree. It's also believed to be 2,500 years old. This tree holds the record for being the largest living thing on earth. It's not the tallest tree in the world, but it's the largest by sheer volume. How did it get that way? It kept growing, year after year. I'm going somewhere with this.

There is a tree that holds another record. It's called the Methuselah tree. You might guess the record based on its namesake. It's the oldest (non-clonal) organism on earth. It's the oldest living tree in the world. Look at the picture some time, it looks like the definition of gnarly. The interesting thing is that the Methuselah tree is not that big. It's a good sized tree but considering it is over 4,800 years old you'd think it would be huge. This thing was a seedling shortly after Noah landed his Ark, unless it was already growing before and survived the flood.

This tree should be enormous but it stands around 60 feet tall. I have trees taller than that in my yard. What's the difference between Methuselah and General

Sherman? Why did one grow so large and the other, even though it was older, didn't grow? The answer is found in their environments. The Methuselah tree grows in a harsh landscape, it's not concerned so much with growth as it is with survival. It's just trying to stay alive, and it's doing a good job at it but there is not much growth.

Let me get to the point. In life and in ministry you can grow or you can survive. Just because you're alive doesn't mean you're growing. Just because you chalk up another year of ministry doesn't mean you had any noticeable growth in your life. Like a tree there may be years of noticeable growth in your life and others where there doesn't seem to be anything happening. It's up to you to decide to keep growing. It all depends on your soil.

In order to grow, you need a healthy environment. Surround yourself with things that will feed you mentally, physically and spiritually. Take purposeful steps to engage yourself in activities that promote growth. Growth is never easy. In fact where there is a lot of growth at once it is painful. As adults we probably don't remember but there is pain associated with growth. It's called growing pains. Your bones and joints ache, your body feels sore, because it's growing.

In our society we have an education mentality. By that I mean we go to school and get our education. Maybe we take classes at night or go to college and get a degree. When we start a job, we might get training for a few days or weeks to do a job. For most people that is where the education stops. We learn what we need to know and the learning stops. But to communicate effectively we need to become people who never stop growing.

> "IF IN PREACHING THE GOSPEL YOU SUBSTITUTE YOUR KNOWLEDGE OF THE WAY OF SALVATION FOR CONFIDENCE IN THE POWER OF THE GOSPEL, YOU HINDER PEOPLE FROM GETTING TO REALITY."
> -Oswald Chambers

Think of it this way, how boring would it be if you never learned anything new the rest of your life. If all you would ever know is what you have learned up to this point in life think how dull your preaching would be. It wouldn't take long to use up the information you currently know. You would have plateaued. You don't have any new stories, just the same old tired illustrations. No new insight from the Word of God. But even more you're still the same person you were when you started out. You haven't grown as a person. You are just surviving, but you were created to thrive.

The Law of Growth isn't just about preaching but it's about you as a person. Because here's the thing, no one wants to come out week after week and listen to a person who is just surviving at life. You need to learn how to thrive, for yourself and as an example to the people you are ministering to. Your communication, your preaching, goes beyond the pulpit and into your daily life. The way you live is your greatest sermon, so live well. Live like God intended you to live. Thrive.

> "YOU CANNOT GO BACK AND CHANGE THE BEGINNING, BUT YOU CAN START WHERE YOU ARE AND CHANGE THE ENDING."
>
> -C.S. Lewis

THREE AREANS OF LIFE

There are three main arenas of your life. You live in a body and you have what we call a soul (we will define that as your mind, will and emotions). But you are not your body and you are not your soul. You are a spirit. That's the part of you that has come alive when you were born again. When you made Jesus your Lord life entered your spirit and now your spirit will live eternally with Him. So you have three parts. Obviously your spirit man is the most important arena, but that doesn't mean we ignore the other areas of our lives.

We need to have visible growth in every arena. We should be growing spiritually in our walk with the Lord. That's your intimate time with Him. Just like you grow in a relationship with a person we should grow in our relationship with Him. If you are married, you should know your spouse better at this moment than you did when you first met. How did that happen? Through conversations, walks on the beach, long dinners, laughing together and the list goes on. You did things with each other. The more you were with the other person the more you got to know them. Rings. Growth lines in your relationship life. That's what we're looking for in our spiritual walk. Not for the sake of pointing at a ring and showing everyone our growth. No, this is for us. We need this. We need Him.

This carries on into the soul arena, the area of our minds. Just like we need to be growing spiritually we need to be growing mentally. Good communicators are readers. Extra points to you if you made it this far in the book that means you are a learner. We need to be learning new things, it will carry over into your communication. When you read an incredible story, you will have ideas to use in your messages. Beyond that this thing called your mind is like a muscle. The more you use it the stronger it gets. It takes a strong mind to communicate well. It takes a lot of mental work to put together a message but if that's the only workout your mind gets in a week it will get dull quick. You need to keep that thing sharp.

The stronger your mind is the better you will communicate. I don't mean you need to be an intellectual to preach. But you need to be sharp. Maybe while you're preaching you want to jump into a topic in a different way than you prepared, it takes a sharp mind to do that and not get lost.

The third arena is one of the hardest for many people that's the arena of your body. If you don't keep your body in check you won't be around to keep preaching and some people will look at you, think you're a mess and won't hear what you have to say. But again, while this chapter is important to our overall communication it's less about that and more about becoming the best version of ourselves we can be. When we live right, we are bringing glory to God. He wants us to take care of ourselves. He's given us these bodies to last our entire lives on this earth so we need to take care of them.

I don't even have to write these words, you already know you need to eat right and exercise. Let me share my experience briefly. I was in my twenties and was a youth pastor. My schedule was full all day long and so I thought I was too busy to exercise. I wasn't eating right and put on some weight. Before I knew it I had back pain. The first time it happened I was in bed for a couple days unable to walk. This would happen on and off for years until one day I went to see a doctor.

The doctor looked me in the eye and said, "There is nothing wrong with your back." I was sitting there thinking about finding a second opinion when he chimed in again, "Your muscles are just too weak to support your body. You need to exercise."

I didn't want to hear that, but I knew I didn't want pain anymore so I took his advice. At first it was hard. I didn't think I had time for exercise but I realized when I was laying in bed in pain and not able to walk that was much worse. So I made time. The more I exercised the more I enjoyed it. There is a scientific explanation but simply put, a chemical is released in your brain when you exercise that becomes like a drug. You start to crave it. It goes from being a burden to being something you want to do. And when I began exercising, I found my mind was sharper. I could think clearer and I felt better.

If you don't exercise regularly find something you enjoy that you can do several days a week. I love lifting weights and biking. Find something you enjoy and stick to it. Get on a healthy eating lifestyle, not a diet. We can't take care of our bodies for a few months and then go back to whatever mess we were doing before. Make changes that will last for your lifetime.

"WE CANNOT BECOME WHAT WE WANT BY REMAINING WHAT WE ARE."

-Max Depree

Take care of yourself. Grow. You may not see the growth all the time. It's hard to notice the growth of a tree. But when it's cut down the growth is obvious. You might never notice all the growth you've had over the course of your life but one day everything will become obvious.

NUTS & BOLTS

- *Evaluate and set goals*

    Take a good hard look at your life. Spend some time thinking about the three arenas: spiritual, mental and physical. Are you experiencing consistent growth in all three areas? Choose a weekly, monthly and annual goal for each area. Record these goals in your journal or some place you will see them often.

- *Put your schedule to work*

    Choose a time each week for you to review your goals and adjust them as necessary. Take out your calendar and block out times for you to accomplish your goals. Give yourself adequate time and don't schedule anything else during this time. You need this.

- *Celebrate*

    Every time you hit a goal go ahead and celebrate. It might remind you of Pavlov's dog but that's ok, we like rewards, it helps keep us motivated.

THE LAW OF THE BELL
Good communicators become great with time, never give up

One of the most physically challenging programs I have ever heard of is the Navy Seal program. Those who finish the school are the best of the best. During training the recruits are constantly moving. They are given little sleep, just a few hours toward the end of their training. By they end they can't even seem to remember a time when they weren't cold, wet or muddy.

During the time they call "Hell Week" their instructor is encouraging them with a simple message. Quit. Just quit. How's that for encouragement? He tells them they could go home and sleep. They could go on vacation some place warm. If they dropped out, they could be dry. They could shower and wash the mud out of their ears if they just quit. A large brass bell hangs in the center of the camp for everyone to see. If they want to quit all they have to do is walk up to that bell and give it a ring.

The instructor urges them, "Go ring the bell. This is too hard. You'll never make it. You're not good enough to be here. That other guy quit already. Just quit."

Only the best of the best make it through that training to become Navy Seals. The temptation to quit is just too strong. Even though all of those guys want nothing more than to finish, some of them just can't do it.

When you preach there are times, you will be tempted to ring the bell. You might hear the voice of the enemy in the back of your mind saying, "It's too hard. Drop out, you'll never make it. You're not good enough." It doesn't matter if you've been preaching for years, that voice still comes. There will be high moments, that's for sure but there are also low points. It's how you handle the low times that will determine if you keep going.

Those low times are the times the voice is the strongest. *QUIT. RING THE BELL.* This may seem like a strange law. How does this law make me a better preacher? It's simple. If you quit you won't be a very good preacher. You need to recognize there is an enemy who wants nothing more than to destroy your life and stop you from preaching the Word of God. Every time you go through a valley of frustration, he's there to tell you to give up. What do you do?

Too many preachers have given up out of frustration. Sometimes it feels like we're not making a difference and it's tempting to give up. Sometimes it feels like we're preaching and no one is listening, why should I keep going? When I preach my heart out and no one responds I must not be in the right job.

There have been times I have felt like quitting. For

me it was always during an frustrating moment. How do you handle those moments? The only reason I kept going was that I knew God had called me and I hadn't heard Him tell me to quit.

This book is all about helping you to become the best communicator, and the best preacher you can be. But preaching is a unique profession. It can be rewarding and in the very next moment overwhelming. You can literally go from, "I have the greatest job in the world!" to "I hate my job," in a heartbeat.

"THERE ARE FAR, FAR BETTER THINGS AHEAD THAN ANY WE HAVE BEHIND."

-C.S. Lewis

THE WEAPONS OF OUR WARFARE

I want to share some encouragement with you to keep going. As I mentioned the enemy is all too happy to tell you to quit when you're going through a frustrating moment. I don't want to give him too much credit after all he is a defeated foe. But we need to understand how he operates. He has a motive, and that is to silence you. But we have weapons at our disposal to use against the enemy. Look at what it says in 2 Corinthians 10:3-5

> *For though we walk in the flesh, we do not war after the flesh:*

> (For the weapons of our warfare are not carnal, but mighty through God to the pulling down of strong holds;)
>
> Casting down imaginations, and every high thing that exalteth itself against the knowledge of God, and bringing into captivity every thought to the obedience of Christ; (KJV)

It says we do not have worldly weapons; we have weapons that are powerful through God. Imagine some worldly weapons: machine guns, grenade launchers, tomahawk missiles, our weapons aren't like those. We have powerful weapons. Look at what he said those weapons are powerful for, they pull down or demolish strongholds. A stronghold was like a fortress. It was walled and secure. There were soldiers guarding it. No one was getting inside. But our weapons demolish strongholds.

He informs us what the strongholds are. It says we cast down imaginations, in another translation it says, "arguments." Now what kind of thing is that? He says we have weapons that are mightier than anything this world has ever seen. But our weapons demolish arguments and imaginations?

Think back to the Garden of Eden for a minute. What did the enemy do there? He asked Eve questions. His questions were meant to stir up conflict inside of her. He asks things like, "Did God really say…?" Then he tells her things contrary to what God said. "No you won't die." He's stirring up arguments inside her. His goal is to get her to imagine what it could be like if she ate the fruit. He tells her she won't die, but instead she will be like God. The lie gets inside her head and grows in her imagination.

God gave us something incredible called an imagination. It lets us create things. We couldn't build a building if we first couldn't imagine what it would look like. The imagination is a powerful tool but also a dangerous place. The enemy likes to go to work in the imagination. He knows if he can control how you think, he will control your life. It's in the imagination where arguments, strife, discontentment, and insecurity begin.

I heard a story about a salesman who was traveling through the countryside late one night. He was in the middle of nowhere when a tire blew out. He pulled to the side of the dirt road and bent down to look at the ruined tire just as the rain started. The man popped his trunk and dug around for his tools. That's when he realized his lug wrench was missing.

He remembered seeing a farmhouse about a mile back and went ask if he could borrow the tool. As he walked in the dark, his mind wandered. What would the farmer think of being woken up in the middle of the night? Would he want to help him at this late hour, in the rain? He imagined how the conversation would go. He would holler up at his window while the man was warm in bed, refusing to help. The more he thought about it the more upset he got. He was sure the farmer would not help him.

When he got to the house he was soaking wet and mad as a hornet. He pounded on the man's door. The farmer opened an upstairs window and asked who was there, just like the man was expecting.

"You know darn well who it is!" the man shouted. "I

want you to know I don't even want your help. I wouldn't use your stupid lug wrench if it was the last one on earth." Then the man turned around and stomped back off into the night.

It's a funny story but there is truth to it. So much of our frustration comes out of our imagination. We think someone is upset and we imagine a reason. Before you know it we're convinced they're angry with us, until we find out they're not. They didn't even know there was a problem. Sometimes we read into a situation and imagine what's going on. We get our feelings hurt. We imagine what people think of our preaching. You see the danger. If we're not careful, we'll wind up like that salesman.

But we have power to tear down imaginations. That's your imagination, when it wants to go in a direction contrary to what the Lord says. We have weapons to tear down that thing, our weapon is the Word of God. When my imagination says, "I'm no good." I have to say, "Wait a minute. He's made me the righteousness of God in Christ." When my imagination says, "I can't do it." I need to stand up and say, "I can do all things through Christ who gives me strength."

We have power over our imaginations and every thought, word or action that is contrary to what God's Word says. That's power right there. A man is controlled by his thoughts. Just like a bit can turn a horse a thought can change the direction of your life. That's why when a thought comes that isn't from above you need to take authority over it. We should not be controlled by our thoughts but by His thoughts about us. The verse above said we should take those thoughts captive. Treat them like prisoners of war. Lock them up and don't listen to them. They're there to deceive and mislead. Instead we should be led by the Holy Spirit.

26.2

Let me close out this chapter with a word about endurance. It says in Hebrews 12:1-2

> *Therefore, since we also have such a large cloud of witnesses surrounding us, let us lay aside every weight and the sin that so easily ensnares us. Let us run with endurance the race that lies before us, keeping our eyes on Jesus, the source and perfecter of our faith, who for the joy that lay before Him endured a cross and despised the shame and has sat down at the right hand of God's throne.*

He talks about a cloud of witnesses. The cloud he is referring to are those who have gone before us, the "heroes of faith," mentioned in Hebrews 11. They're watching to see what we will do at this moment in history. It's a little overwhelming to think all of heaven is watching what we're doing. So he says because of this we need to lay aside sin and anything that would distract us from our goal so we can run.

He compares our lives to a race, and he tells us to run with endurance. This life isn't a sprint. It's a marathon. I've met people who run marathons. They make me feel so out of shape. These athletes literally run every day. They are constantly training. Some days they will run five or ten miles or more just to keep up their endurance. Why do they do this? Why put yourself through that kind of torture? There is a goal in mind and they know if they don't keep running they'll never make it the entire 26.2 miles. They don't want to drop early. The goal isn't to start the race and have to quit or to run 25 miles just to pass out before the finish line. They are training to finish the race.

He tells us here to run the race with endurance. Keep going. If you fall down, get up. It doesn't matter what you've been through. If you've struggled, if you've fallen if you feel washed up if people have criticized you… keep going. When you feel like you've fallen down, get up. All of heaven is watching to see how you will live and they're cheering you on. Most of all your life is being played out for an audience of one. He's the only one who matters. What he thinks of you is the only opinion that counts.

"PAUL NEVER DEVELOPED A NEGATIVE ATTITUDE. HE PICKED HIS BLOODY BODY UP OUT OF THE DIRT AND WENT BACK INTO THE CITY WHERE HE HAD ALMOST BEEN STONED TO DEATH, AND HE SAID, 'HEY ABOUT THAT SERMON I DIDN'T FINISH PREACHING - HERE IT IS!"

-John Hagee

Keep your eyes on Him. He is the author, and he is the perfecter of our faith. I hope this chapter encouraged you. Learn the Law of the Bell. Keep going no matter what. Never give up.

NUTS & BOLTS

- *Encourage yourself*

    The Word of God says that David encouraged himself in the Lord. There were seasons he went through where he needed encouragement and he knew there was only one place to get it. We need to get good at encouraging ourselves in the Lord. Find encouraging Scriptures and post them around your office. Or even better memorize them and recite them to yourself. Get good at casting all your cares on Him.

- *Get good at running*

    Determine to keep going no matter what. Marathon runners push themselves when they're tired, when the weather's bad, when they feel like quitting, they keep going. Run like that. Keep going. Determine to push yourself even when you don't want to.

THANK YOU

Thanks for reading my book. My prayer is that it was an encouragement for you and a practical tool to help you develop your communication skills.

I'd love to hear from you. If you have questions, or would like to see the video series that goes along with this book you can do that at:

lawsofcommunication.weebly.com

If you need some specific help with your preaching I'd love to be a resource for you. You may contact me through my website for a personal coaching session.

If you enjoyed the book be sure to leave me a review! God bless.

APPENDIX

There are some great preaching and study resources out there. You probably have some you like. I didn't want to make an exhaustive list but just give you a few of the ones I use on a regular basis.

PRINT RESOURCES

Jamison, Fausset & Browns (Commentary)

Matthew Henry (Commentary)

Vines Expository Dictionary

Strongs (of course)

There are some terrific apps and websites that have these resources and a lot more. If you don't have these books you can find some of them for free and they take up a lot less space on your bookshelf.

APPS

Olive Tree – This is a free app. Inside the app they have tons of books you can download to your library. Some of the books will cost you but some are free. With this app you can have your Bible open and next to the passage you can have open a parallel version or a commentary. I love this app and use it constantly even when I'm not doing study for a message.

CBN Bible – If you're looking for a free version of Strongs this has it. It's simple to look up any word in any passage and get the Hebrew or Greek and the meaning of the word. I also use this one a lot.

ONLINE

Biblehub.com - There are some great websites and you might have one you like better but I always find myself using this one. It has the commentaries and Strongs. It's easy to do word studies, etc.

ENDNOTES

[1] J.K. Johnston, Why Christians Sin, (Discovery House, 1992)

[2] Exodus 34:35

[3] 2 Corinthians 3:13

[4] I Corinthians 11:1

[5] Robert P. Dungan, Jr., Winning the New Civil War, (Multnomah Books, 1991), p. 38.

[6] Lewis Carroll, *Alice's Adventures in Wonderland,* (Broadview Press, Peterborough, Ont, 2000)

[7] I Corinthians 9:22

[8] Mark Byrnes "How The London Bridge Ended Up in Arizona," Citylab.com, October 10, 2013, CityLab https://www.citylab.com/design/2013/10/how-original-london-bridge-ended-arizona/7200/

[9] Leah Goldman and Gus Lubin, "The 25 Worst Mistakes in History," April 26, 2011, Business Insider, http://www.businessinsider.com/worst-mistakes-in-history-2011-4?op=1/

[10] "Moody – The Mistake of Not Giving an Invitation," Family Times, http://www.family-times.net/illustration/Unbelief/201340/

[11] Sean Greene, "In 2016 Scientist Discovered 18,000 New Species. Now Meet the Top 10," Los Angeles Times, May 22, 2017, http://www.latimes.com/science/sciencenow/la-sci-sn-new-species-top-10-20170522-htmlstory.html

[12] Aoxue W., "10 Recently Discovered Animals with Amazing Features," Listverse, February 12, 2016, https://listverse.com/2016/02/12/10-recently-discovered-animals-with-amazing-features/

[13] Shel Silverstein, Where the Sidewalk Ends: The Poems & Drawings of Shel Silverstein, (New York: Harper and Row, 1974)

[14] Marvin Maupin, It's Better to Die Laughing than to be Dead Serious, (Bloomington: Author House, 2010), page 87

[15] Proverbs 17:22

[16] C.S. Lewis, C.S. Lewis' Letters to Children, Lyle W. Dorsett and Marjorie Lamp Meade, eds., (New York; Touchstone)

[17] Luke 10:25-29

[18] Adapted from: Wayne Rice, Hot Illustrations for Youth Talks, (Zondervan, 2001), page 105

[19] This story is found in 2 Samuel 12:1-14

[20] Joshua 24:15 (KJV)

[21] Acts 2:37

[22] See I Samuel 17:33-36

[23] From notes taken on a Ray Lewis interview on CBS morning show (October 2015)

[24] (Halford E. Luccock, Unfinished Business, (Harper & Brothers, 1956)

[25] Luke 4:16-21

[26] Genevieve Shaw Brown, "It's a Small World: 9 Little-Known Facts," ABC News, March 21, 2014, http://abcnews.go.com/Travel/disneys-small-world-facts/story?id=22990670

Made in United States
Troutdale, OR
03/04/2024